Growing Up in the 1950s

Just Seven Blocks
from the
Mexican Border

. . .

A Southern Arizona Memoir

Paul Nichols

INHER|TANCE
PRESS

— For my kids

Michael • Marcie • Amy

and grandkids —

Meghan • Mike • Sean • Nicholas • Jake • Joshua •
Darby • Benjamin • Mari

Dedication

Gloria, my wife, inspiration and encouragement,
I cheerfully dedicate this book to you.

Acknowledgements

To the good people of Arizona, Cochise County, Douglas, Douglas schools and the First Baptist Church. All my blessings are founded upon the good life you built for me.

• • •

A la buena gente de Agua Prieta, Sonora, Mexico: Muchas gracias por su respeto a mi padre ("Hermano Pablo") y a mi familia. Nos han dado amor y gracia...y memorias duraderas.

Table of Contents

Introduction..1
Douglas, Arizona..3
You Can't Tell The Players Without A Scorecard..............................8
It Was Already Past My Bedtime 11
Next, 1123 Seventh Street...14
Adventures at 1122 Seventh Street 17
Our House. Come On In...19
1122 Seventh. One Cool House. 22
The Story of Mom's Whistle..25
Wide Streets and Other Playgrounds 28
Fight! Fight!...32
Vacant Lots...34
Noel and Mr. Whitemule...36
The Neatest Driveway on Earth 38
Friend of the Bees, Part 1..42
Friend of the Bees, Part 2..44
Slaughter's Ranch..46
We Were Out Where the Sky is Big...50
In Our Back Yard We Recycled...52
Neatly Stacked Lumber in Our Back Yard...55
Famous Tree Houses in Our Back Yard..57
A Big "X" Marks the Spot in Our Back Yard......................................59
Toys for Boys (Tools) in Our Back Yard 61
Chickens and Other Fowl Things in Our Back Yard 63
How To Pluck A Chicken in Our Back Yard..65
The Sweet and Sticky Garage in Our Back Yard.................................67
We Fired Up Burn Barrels in Our Back Yard 71
Eunice's Barrel Began in Our Back Yard...73
Dangerous Supers Barrel in Our Back Yard 76
Dad's Garden(s) in Our Back Yard..78
The Shed in Our Back Yard 80
The Sound of Sunrise...83
Two Sweet Women 85
God Bless America 87
Only Three Dozen Chocolate Chip Cookies 89
Big Brothers! What Good Are They? 91
Saturday Afternoon Matinees 93
God's Will for Your Life for Just $6...96

Do Not Try This At Home! 99
A Match Made in Agua Prieta 101
Border Wars 105
Douglas Dump 107
Rainy Days 110
Polio in Douglas 114
You Know Why They Shoot Horses, Don't You? 116
The Last Batter 119
The Good, The Bad and The Ugly 124
The Fifth Greatest Day in the History of the World 129
Dairy Queen Rides 132
The Haunted House on Ninth Street 134
Five in the Morning 136
Technicolors for Grandmother 139
Church Services on Seventh Street 142
The Prettiest Girl in Douglas 144
Neal's Wedding 147
Trips Out of Douglas 150
Yes! Virginia! 154
Debbie, Cozette and Valerie—and Jeannine 157
Burma Shave Signs 160
Deep in the Heart of Kansas 162
The Tall Part of Dad 166
The Dimmer Part of Dad 168
Dances With Wolves and Sleeps With Snakes 170
Was Mrs. Ward Left-handed? 175
It Was David Bond 177
Coach Sharp Had Only One Rule 180
The Douglas High School Bulldogs 183
Four Easy Steps Through Douglas High School 187
Beer Cans Galore 190
Joe and Joe and Dad and Mr. Jackson 194
D Day 197
First at Douglas High School 201
G Avenue 203
The Joy of Color 206
Graduation Ceremonies at Douglas High School 211
Mrs. Nichols 212
Nick 217
The Beautiful and Historical First Baptist Church 222
Miscellaneous Quirks 228
We Were Not Poor 237

What Do You Want to be When You Grow Up?..241
Half the Fun of Christmas..242
The Last Day at 1122 Seventh Street...247
One Last Soft Touch..248
Friend of the Bees, Part 3...249
What Ever Happened to...?..252
Epilogue: The Star of the Show...256
Take a Tour of Cochise County...258

.

Introduction

"...out in the stillness of the hot desert; out where no one heard us or saw us. Out where the sky is big and the noonday sun never moves. Out where breezes are forbidden; where heat wins every argument. Out where the rocky ground is sharp and hot. Out where the spirit of the great Apaches follows you along the desert floor. Out where water is only a mirage and shade comes only at night. Out where everything is about a hundred miles from here.

Ah, the Southern Arizona desert. What a great place. What a special place!"

• • •

I'm proud to say that I grew up in Douglas, Cochise County, Arizona, a wild and wonderful place for boys with a Huck Finn sense of adventure. Huck Finn would have loved Cochise County. It's right next to Mexico. We didn't have a magnificent river like he had, but he never watched a puma bound across the hot, rocky desert. Nor did he ever drink cool artesian water while it bubbled straight up out of the hot desert dirt. I did both.

Unfortunately, our kids grew up in the Northwest, so I told them stories about growing up at 1122 Seventh Street, Douglas, Arizona—1943 to 1960. Wouldn't you know it? They grew up and had kids of their own. They brought them over to the house and said, "Dad, tell 'em about the time that you..."

When I was growing up, we asked, "Tell us a story, Dad, 'bout when you were a little boy."

He told me, my brothers, sister and cousins some great stories about his youth—1904 to 1920-something. One of my older cousins pleaded with him time and again to write down his stories. "Or at least let me record them, Nick. You can just talk." He always declined. "Naw. That's just the way we lived," he excused. "Nobody cares about how I grew up." Well, yes we did care. In fact, I still want to know more about my dad.

1

I want my kids to know more about me, too. When they left home, I kept some typewritten notes about growing up in the Southern Arizona Desert. Then came the computer and the notes became little stories. The little stories became a book—for my kids and grandkids. This is it. It's part of their roots.

"There are two lasting bequests we can give our children: One is roots, the other is wings."

—Hodding Carter, 1907–1972,
American author and newspaperman

Douglas, Arizona

A group of us Douglas High School alumni were huddled together one October evening not long ago, reminiscing about our home town. Someone said, "Douglas is in your blood."

Someone else said, "If you only live here for just a few years, it gets in your blood, too."

And, "If you marry someone from Douglas, it'll get in your blood sooner or later."

"But to graduate from Douglas High School..." she said dreamily.

"Hey! Looka my shirt," he puffed. "What does it say?"

"Once a Bulldog...always a Bulldog!" we read together.

"Alright then!"

"Let's drink to that!"

And let's talk about that, too. Douglas—as it was in the 1950s.

When you approached Douglas from the northwest (coming out of Bisbee) it was easy to see D Hill on the far side of town. It was clearly seen from 25 miles away—if you squinted. D Hill is so named because it boasts a huge white "D" near its top. Many towns in the western states feature the same thing, but Douglas' D is the most impressive of them all. The sun also rises from behind D Hill.

Immediately after rounding the bend that leads out of Bisbee, a panoramic view of the Sulphur Springs Valley rises up. No two views are ever the same, but Highway 80 is part of it. America has some magnificent scenery and the view looking down from Bisbee over that valley ranks among the best, if you ask me.

After just a few more miles, there is the whole of Douglas and its Mexican neighbor, Agua Prieta, Sonora, Mexico. They're spread out in the valley from north to south. At night, the two twinkling towns are a lake of lights. It's pretty: those lights shimmering like the Lord's own diamonds. Maybe that's why they call it "God's Country."

Bisbee is a "mile high" city nestled in the Mule Mountains of Cochise County. It sits about a thousand feet higher than Douglas, which is why Douglas is so easy to see from so far away.

Douglas was founded in 1901 (I think) as a fine flat place to smelt all that copper dug out of Bisbee. It's in the remote southeastern corner of Arizona, in Cochise County, about 30 miles on a line to New Mexico. Its southern city limit is the US–Mexico border.

From the '20s to the '80s, there was no mistaking the copper smelter in Douglas with its towering black and white smoke stacks. Stinky, gray-white clouds of sulphur smoke poured out of those stacks twenty-four hours a day, where copper was smelted after it was taken from the Lavender Pit in Bisbee and trained downhill to the smelter.

When you reached Douglas, you passed right in front of the smelter. It was impressive. Rightly so: it was there from the early 1900s and the slag ring (the waste dumped around the smelter) built up for all those years. If you passed the smelter at night, when slag was dumped, the whole black night lit up bright, bright orange. Sometimes it was beautiful; sometimes it was scary. Every time was impressive.

You "officially" arrived in Douglas when you slowed to 25 MPH and drove through the underpass onto G Avenue.

The approach to Douglas from the other north, from Lordsburg, New Mexico, is not as dramatic. However, some terrific craggy mountains greets travelers not far from town. Then there were a few sweeping curves and suddenly—Douglas just sorta showed up. And almost without knowing it, there you were on A Avenue.

• • •

Please Note Department: the only way *in* to Douglas is from the north. The only way *out* is to the north—unless you want to escape to Mexico, which ain't a bad idea.

• • •

Wide streets. Everyone who visits Douglas comments on the wide streets. And they're straight, too. Douglas was originally laid out in a one-mile grid. Every eight streets equals one mile. They say that the streets were originally made wide enough to turn around a team of twenty mules.

Park cars on both sides of the street and there's still plenty of room for two-way traffic—and a great, noisy football game. Kids love the wide streets, too. "Okay, Mr. Green's car is the goal line on that end, and Mr. Brown's bush is the goal line down there."

Unfortunately, there are no beautiful tree-lined streets. I guess that's the way it is in the desert. Fortunately, there are no potholes in those wide streets. That's a good thing.

Cochise County is well-known for the "Shootout at OK Corral" in Tombstone starring Doc Holliday, Wyatt Earp and the Clanton boys. Apache Indian Chiefs Cochise and Geronimo called Cochise County their homeland. Something "new" was discovered in Cochise County not long after we moved away. The Kartchner Caverns at Benson were discovered in 1974, underground caverns as beautiful and impressive as any in the world. It may be that they are eventually connected to the Carlsbad Caverns in New Mexico. Wouldn't that be something?

Cochise County, Arizona. Looking northeast from Geronimo Trail and the Airport Park in Douglas, 2008. It looks like it might rain any minute. Or not.

Oh, and this is special. Whenever you're in Bisbee, be sure to drive by the Warren Ballpark. Built in 1909, *it's the oldest baseball park-stadium in the US.* How 'bout them apples! Right there in Cochise County. Who woulda thunk it?

Before Arizona was a state, Douglas was wilder and more wicked than Tombstone ever was. Back then saloons and brothels were the first order of business. The infamous Mexican bandit Pancho Villa made a couple of sorties into Douglas, and when I was a boy Dad showed me some bullet holes that Pancho and his gangs left behind in a few of Douglas' adobe buildings. The famous Texas Ranger-rancher-gunfighter-politician-businessman-community leader, John Slaughter, lived near Douglas and died there in 1922.

Right next to Douglas is Pirtleville, a tiny town of several Mexican families. Its cemetery faces south—toward Mexico, the only cemetery in the US that does so. All the other American cemeteries point east. That little cemetery was once featured in a *Ripley's Believe It or Not* book.

Immediately below the Mexican border is Agua Prieta, Sonora, Mexico. It used to be a small town. Now it's bigger than Douglas.

Whether you were entering Mexico or coming out, it was pretty likely you saw my dad, an Immigration officer there in Douglas' Port of Entry, "the Port." He worked there for thirty-seven years.

Because of its location there on the border, it's only natural that most of Douglas' citizens are Mexican people. Beautiful people, every one. Half of my friends were Mexicans. My nickname is *Pablito*, given to me by who-knows-who when I was just a little tyke. To this day, when I make new Mexican acquaintances, it's not long before they call me *Pablito*, "Little Paul."

Historically, Douglas boasts the Gadsden Hotel, which is listed in the *National Register of Historic Places.* Outside it's plain. Inside it's beautiful. Paul Newman majestically descended its grand marble staircase in the movie, *The Life and Times of Judge Roy Bean.* And legend has it that Pancho Villa rode his horse up those same steps.

The first time I ever watched TV was in the lobby of the Gadsden Hotel. A rather large group of people were invited to see the first television broadcast into Douglas. I was twelve and we watched part of a western movie. Three or four years later my parents bought a TV that didn't work. We rarely watched it.

Speaking of movies and grand staircases, The Grand Theatre in Douglas was once one of the most beautiful theaters west of the Mississippi. It was built in 1919 and helped Douglas shake some of its not-so-attractive past. Anna Pavlova, the world renown Russian ballerina, actress Ginger Rogers and even the great march king, John Phillip Sousa performed on stage in The Grand Theatre, at the corner of Twelfth Street and G Avenue. It's a masterful piece of architecture; currently under renovation (2009).

Douglas opened the first international airport in the entire western hemisphere, dedicated by Eleanor Roosevelt in 1933. Yes, the first. It was international because the runway ran right into Mexico. It's still an active little airport, but a border fence runs across the runway now. Amelia Earhart landed in Douglas a time or two, too.

I grew up believing that Douglas was also the home of the world's first Motor Hotel, or Mo-Tel. Other towns and cities across the country make the same claim, but I heard it on a Paul Harvey radio show a long, long time ago. I'll believe anything that Paul Harvey said. I guess.

One day in 1926, Aimee Semple McPherson, a beautiful, charismatic and popular Pentecostal evangelist and founder of the Four Square Gospel denomination, walked into Douglas from Agua Prieta. She claimed that she had escaped from some kidnappers. That made scandalous national headlines because most people had decided she had drowned while swimming at a California beach. Had she pulled off a great hoax? The question remains to this day.

Stan Jones wrote the well-known cowboy song "Ghost Riders in the Sky" after an evening up on D Hill. He grew up in Douglas and ended up in the Country Music Hall of Fame.

Just after I left Douglas for the army, the playwright and novelist, Thornton Wilder came to town and almost adopted Douglas.

"Be exalted, O God, above the heavens and let your glory be over all the earth."

—Psalm 108:5

You Can't Tell The Players Without A Scorecard

- **Doug Foster**, and his younger brothers, **Mike** and **Jimmy**, lived on the far corner of the block at 1198 Seventh Street. Doug was my best friend from infancy through high school. He went to college, med school, military. He did some volunteer missionary work in the Pacific. Then he opened his doctor's office in Douglas—his life-long dream. He was my mom's doctor for a little while. I'm a month older than Doug.

- **Armando Contreras** lived next door to Doug at 1194 Seventh Street. Armando had a couple of older brothers about Neal and Noel's ages. He had a baby sister who was born when we were about 12. She was already an aunt.

- **Luis de la Vara**, and his older brothers, **Eddie** and **Ruben**. Eddie had a mental defect, but I never realized it. He was Neal's age, I think, and he always called me "Grampa." Why? I don't know, but he always laughed when he said it. Eddie was an excellent artist. He sat on his front porch and painted some really good neighborhood scenes. Ruben was a year or two younger than Noel. It was Luis, though, who played with us.

- **George Kaine** lived next door to us and was Noel's age; Noel's friend.

- **Leonard Heuberger** lived across the street at 1109.

- **Richie Verdugo** lived behind us on Eighth Street.

- **Lawson** and **Jonnie Barret** lived at 1123 (our previous residence). Lawson was called Butch most of the time.

- **Luis** and **Ruben Rodriguez** lived on Fourth Street.

- **Ernesto Valenzuela** lived in the 1000 block, sort of caddy-corner from us.

- **Billy Duncan** lived a couple of houses down from the Valenzuela's.

- **Joe Pinedo** lived on Sixth Street. In high school he gave me and Joe Tippy a ride to school every day. (**Joe Tippy** lived on International Avenue, which was just eight feet from the Mexican border.)

- **George Early**. His father owned the grocery store across from the Fosters. They lived in that store, too, in an attached apartment.

- **Hollis Phillips** moved to Douglas from Bisbee about age 12. We played a couple of summers together on a Babe Ruth baseball team. He was one of the best baseball players that Douglas ever produced.

- **Rudy Campos**. His father built the house at 1125, ruining one great vacant lot-playground-sandlot baseball field.

- **Carlos** and **Ruben Guido**. They lived on our street about seven years at 1157. Mr. Guido was an official in the Mexican Ambassador's local office.

- **Steve Whitehead** lived across "The Desert" on Florida Avenue. He often came into our neighborhood to do whatever we were doing. Once in awhile we meandered to his house, usually for a drink of water.

- **Neal** and **Noel**. My brothers. Neal's nine years older than I and Noel is six years older. So I didn't "play" with them a lot. I fussed with them...

If we gathered just a few of those boys on a sunny Saturday morning, we managed to concoct an assortment of wildly daring adventures and unforgettable baseball games.

There were girls, too, of course. My sister **Ruth** led this parade of Miss 7th Street cuties. **Graciella** and **Rose Marie Haro**, **Bette** and **Jeanette Duncan**, **Rose Pinedo**, **Donna Foster**, **Linda**, **Gloria** and **Lolita Barret**, **Patsy Savage**, **Ginny Verdugo**, **Rosela Contreras** and **Judy Phillips**.

9

These are the kids that I played with, rassled with, rascaled with and went to school with most of my early life. Of course, I had many school friends and Sunday School friends, but these are the kids in my immediate neighborhood. From time to time a family moved into, then out of the little home at 1192 next to the Contreras'. That usually meant another playmate. John Matson was the orneriest and most infamous of them all, and often had green teeth. The Matsons left after just a couple of years. Whew!

". . . there is a friend who sticks closer than a brother."

—Proverbs 18:24

It Was Already Past My Bedtime

Well, let's talk about me.

**Earliest known photo of me, with my
Grandmother, Amy Marple. 1943.**

I was born just nine blocks from Mexico during WWII. It was a Saturday night, about 10:25 p.m., February 6, 1943. I was born in Copper Queen Hospital in Douglas, Arizona, where Dr. Arnold Duncan delivered me. It was already past my bedtime.

My parents are **Paul J.** and **Nell A. Nichols**. My brothers are **Neal** and **Noel. Ruth** is my sister. We had a brother older than all of us, Paul Thomas Nichols, who died when he was about eighteen months old. So I can say, "My name is Paul. My brother's name is Paul, too." Neal and Noel are nine and six years older than I. Ruth is three years younger.

My family lived at 925 Sixteenth Street when I was born, and my earliest memories are from that house.

The earliest memory of all is not a pretty one. A monster came into my crib and lowered its face down close to mine. I screamed! Yes, indeed! *Bellowed!* It came down toward my face, lower and lower, hovering over me. Defenseless, I just kept screaming. Suddenly that monster went away, but I was still scared. I'm telling you: if it ever comes back, I'm sure it will gobble me up right where I lay!

I told this monster story to my mother more than once.

"You were nine months old then," she told me. "You had pneumonia."

That "monster" was Dr. Duncan. Doctors made house calls in the 40s. He hovered over me while he examined my eyes and nose and so forth. He wore one of those old eye-hole mirrors that doctors used to clamp to their foreheads.

I don't think doctors should clamp mirrors to their foreheads and run all over town scaring helpless little infants.

My crib was next to a door that led to the front porch, but it wasn't the main front door. Many houses of that era had two front doors. My diaper was changed in that room, on my parent's bed. I once described their yellowish bed spread to Mom. "That's right," she confirmed. "We only had that bed spread for a short time."

I rode my first donkey at 925 Sixteenth and there's a picture to prove it. I was two at the time, on a donkey with Tomas Rodriquez, or "Tommy Next Door." I ate Mexican food at his house. There was a day that I went home after lunch with a full poopie diaper. The diaper got full during lunch and I was uncomfortable! I guess I forgot all about my potty training that day because Mom was waiting for me on the porch with her hands on her hips.

Handsome donkey with Me, Noel, Alejandra and Tommy Rodriguez ("Tommy Next Door")

I spoke fluent Spanish in the Rodriquez' home; that is, as fluent as a two- or three-year-old can speak it. I know this is true, because Tommy's mother didn't speak English and she and I exchanged sentences—in Spanish.

I regret that my Spanish then was a lot better than it is now.

"Feb. 6 Annual leave. Allen Paul Nichols was born this day."

—My dad's diary

Next, 1123 Seventh Street

Noel saw what I had done and ran off to tell Mom. While he was off tattling, I streaked out of the garage, around the house and onto the front porch. I lay low next to a hole in the plaster walls that surrounded our wrap-around porch. Through the hole, I saw them coming. Mom had a belt. And Noel was grinning. It didn't take long to find me.

"What have we told you about mixing the dog food and the chicken feed?" Mom demanded. She grabbed me by the arm and roughly jerked me up from my hiding place. I began screaming and she began spanking. I suppose Noel kept on grinning.

My family lived at 1123 Seventh Street from my age three to five. The rule there was: *Do not mix the dog food and the chicken food*, which were kept in separate barrels out in our dusty garage—next to the chicken coop.

Nobody ever said anything about haircuts, though.

Doug Foster, Armando Contreras and I once gave my sister Ruth quite a haircut outside next to the garage. She was so patient. She sat still and calm and let the three of us five-year-old boys take turns demonstrating the proper way to cut hair.

Once again, when my mother discovered us, she jerked me around and started spanking. I started screaming. Doug and Armando started running.

To this day, my mother hasn't forgiven me that haircut.

At 1123 we had a Collie named Chief. There is a picture or two of me and Chief. Dad had to get rid of him because he bit the mailman—twice. Every school day Chief walked one block to Clawson School with Noel. After Noel crossed the street, Chief ran all the way back to me, leaped upon me and knocked me silly. Every school day this happened. Every school day I encouraged it.

Chief and Me at 1123 Seventh Street.

1123 had a big wrap-around porch, a great place to be during a rain storm. I had a lot of fun on that porch, but not always when we lived there.

Ruth was born while we lived there. Early in the mornings Dad let me give Ruth her bottle. Mom was in bed, Dad and I up and I feeding Ruth. I had to be quiet about it so as not to disturb Mom (as if she didn't know). Ruth slept in my parents' bedroom. Funny, I don't remember where my bed was in that house.

The bathroom. It had two doors, so we walked right through it. In some of today's inexpensive homes, that is called a "continental" bathroom. That bathroom was as large as a decent bedroom. One boring evening I sat in there and put a whole box of white band-aids over all my nicks, scratches and mosquito bites. I proudly showed my mom, who promptly swatted me a few times.

I was a sickling for a spell in that house, too. I don't know what the problem was, but I was in bed for a while. As my family tells it, I kept calling for Neal. In fact, I called so much one time that my folks called him out of school to come home and settle me down. I don't know if that is true or not, but they think it's a great tale.

15

Ruth and I both had the measles in that house. I had the chicken pox there.

I started Kindergarten at 1123, but finished that school year across the street at **1122 Seventh Street.** What a place.

> *". . . and go to the land I will show you."*
>
> —Genesis 12:1

Adventures at 1122 Seventh Street

Our family moved to **1122 Seventh Street** in 1948 when I was five and in Kindergarten. Most all my family values, morals, Christianity and education were developed in that little frame two-bedroom house. Almost all my childhood memories and adventures occurred when we lived at 1122, which is just seven blocks from the Mexican border.

Our front lawn was small and filled with a weed we called "Japanese Clover." It's a vicious weed, with deep roots that require a shovel to remove. It lays hard against the ground and eats up all the grass. It has waxy leaves and produces little burrs that stick to your socks, your pant legs, your dog and anything else that gets close. We had to pick them off before we were allowed in the house. That took awhile sometimes. We didn't play in our little front yard that much.

Two cedar trees graced our front walk. Neal and a couple of his pals invited me out onto the front walk one evening just after a good rain. "There's a nickel under that tree," he told me. "Why don't you get it?" I didn't see any nickel, but down I went to look anyway. The next thing I knew cold rain was pouring down my back. Not really. Neal and his ornery buddies were shaking the wet branches over me.

Me. In front of that cedar tree our first year at 1122 Seventh Street.

The house was white the whole time we lived there. Actually, it was dust-colored, unless we had a really great downpour. Then it was white for a couple of days.

The front porch featured a well-worn tongue-and-groove floor that was hemmed in with "sitting" rails on each end. We got extra shade from a wide trellis of baby roses. My grandmother, when she visited, sat out there for hours and rocked to the sounds of the neighborhood.

I was probably six or seven when I preached a couple of sermons to Ruth and her dolls on that porch. The Lord probably winced when He heard them.

The Neatest Driveway on Earth flowed along the shady side of the house. We got shade from six tall tamarisk trees, and from a long, thick honeysuckle trellis up close to the wall. The back porch, nice and shady in the summer, was a covered concrete slab. There was a long wobbly table out there, but we didn't use it for much. The water cooler was stuck into the back bedroom window, and next to it were three wooden steps leading up to the back screen door.

On the east side of the house was a strip of grass about eight or ten feet wide. Nothing much went on there, except we had to mow it and dig Japanese Clover out of it.

That eastside wall of the house, under the front window, had a big gray patch. Looked like the window had a black eye. The exterior was plaster, but the patch was concrete. It never got painted while we lived there.

This side also featured Mrs. Mason's front lot, an unofficial extension of our yard. From our kitchen window, whenever I did the dishes, I looked out across her lot and up Seventh Street. There was our schoolyard baseball field up at Clawson.

"There's no place like home . . . plate."

—Paul Nichols

Our House. Come On In.

Our living room and dining room were one large room, divided by furniture. Dark green, pull-down shades covered our windows at night. As the years rolled by, they became brittle and tore easily. Dad patched the tears with black friction tape. Why didn't he just buy new shades?

The ceiling tiles were old and dirty, a couple of them sagged and some of them had water stains. Many dreamy times I stared up at those stains and saw alligators or billowing clouds or ships at sea or flowers or anything my imagination discovered. Those stains took me into caves, up mountains, across continents, off to Mars and many other places.

Kids with clean ceilings aren't so lucky.

Probably the first thing you saw when we invited you into our living room was a peaceful and mesmerizing seascape. The moon shone down over a few clouds and over a wide seashore. Neal has that picture in his home now, and it's still as entrancing as when I dreamed into it.

Under the picture our little gas stove warmed the whole house every winter. When it was too cold to hang clothes out on the clothesline, Dad hung a few of them over the stove to dry them—socks and the like.

The dining room kept a nice buffet with matching table and chairs. A tall black piano, always out of tune, haunted the dining room.

Dad kept his typewriter on a metal stand by the big window. There he cranked out our church's Sunday bulletin. Faithfully, faithfully, he prepared it every week onto a long, blue mimeograph stencil. Then on Saturday he'd go down to the church, usually with me and Ruth in tow, and crank out about 100 bulletins. I think there was nothing else he'd rather do—except care for his bees.

Our round dining room table was the main business office, too. Bills were paid there. Newspapers and magazines were read and left there. Mail was dropped there. Dad wrote entries into his diaries and

Mom wrote lengthy letters to relatives. Sometimes sprinkled clothes waited there for ironing. Comic books and small toys got lost there. We kids did our homework there and everybody studied their Sunday School lessons there. We all tried our hands at crafts on that table, and all gifts were wrapped there. Mom pasted S&H Green Stamps and Gold Bond Stamps into their books there.

To do something at the dining room table, we just shoved everything to one side until there was enough table space to do it.

Oh, yes. When we had company, we ate there, too. But we cleaned off the whole table first.

Behind the LR/DR was our Kitchen/Bathroom. We had a big kitchen where we ate our everyday meals on a drop-leaf table. We had some rousing dinners there on that table, first painted white, then gray, pink and finally light green.

Noel burned his arm with hot gravy during dinner once. It took a week of wrap to get him healed.

One evening when Ruth was about eight or nine, she announced at the dinner table that she was pregnant. She really wasn't, but Dad bit his fork in half anyway.

Poor Ruth, she thought she was repeating something cute. Everybody laughed when our older married cousin said it. Ruth didn't even know what pregnant was. At our house, "pregnant" was first cousin to a four-letter word. We always said, "…going to have a baby someday" or "…in a family way."

Our niece Debbie, about a year old, sat in her high chair and smeared a little cottage cheese in her hair one evening. That was good for a laugh from all of us. So she smeared some more, which made for an even bigger, louder laugh. "Well, hey," she thought, "if you liked that, you'll love this! Watch what I can do!" And she dumped the whole bowl on her head, then gleefully rubbed it all through her hair. Yee-haw! What side-splitting fun! A hat made of cottage cheese!

I don't recall much of what Mom ever said at that table except, "If you don't settle down and clean up your plate, young man, I'll part your hair with this table knife."

Ah, but Mom knew how to cook. She made that kitchen smell so terribly good. The original aromatherapy.

A four-legged gas stove not only cooked Mom's meals, but in the winter it contributed to the heat. To get it going, all you had to do was turn on a burner and apply a lit match. A box of Diamond brand stick matches was always on the top shelf.

Many a honey jar was sterilized on that stove. We used a huge pot that held six or eight jars and lots of boiling water. It was so big it required two burners.

Dad brought his soldering iron into the house to heat it on the stove. When it glowed fiery red like a branding iron he hurried outside to solder something. Pretty soon he came back to the stove to fire it up again.

He always lit his pipe there at the stove, too. He'd strike the match on the burner, light up, and then with a deft flick of two fingers, sail the match toward the garbage can. "Zzzzwhiieeerrrrrr," it sang, a little trail of smoke behind it.

No built-in cupboards. We had two or three rolling pantries. Good hiding places for indoor hide-and-seek. We had some open shelves off in a corner where we kept our dinner plates and glasses. Mom decorated up our kitchen one year with a half-dozen aluminum drinking glasses. Each one was a different bright color. Modern progress.

Our garbage can was a painted metal five-gallon bucket. We lined the bottom with a newspaper, then put an open grocery sack in it, too. We kept loaded mouse traps behind it. Once in awhile I had to empty the trap and reset it as part of "taking out the garbage."

Okay, so we lived in a frame house with three inquisitive sons and two gas stoves, a never-ending supply of stick matches, glowing soldering irons, and flaming, zzzzwhiieeerrrr-ing matches that flew into a paper-lined garbage can. How come our house didn't burn down a few times?

Thank you, Lord, for watching over us.

"If you make the Most High your dwelling—even the Lord, who is my refuge—then no harm will befall you, no disaster will come near your tent."

—Psalm 91:9

1122 Seventh. One Cool House.

"Dinner's on the table," Mom called. So everybody got up and fought for the bathroom—which was next to the kitchen. Flush, flush. Wash, wash. Then eat, eat.

That was a cool bathroom. Antiques dealers would pay a ka-zillion dollars for it today. The wooden water tank was over the toilet a few inches below the ceiling, so we pulled a chain to flush. Ever hear the expression, "Who pulled your chain"? The tank was painted to match the rest of the room.

The bathtub stood on four legs and had exposed water pipes at the end of it. It sat directly beneath a high window that, when opened, leaned into the room as far as its little brass chain allowed—about six inches.

Next to the sink hung Dad's razor strop, an intimidating dark brown strip of leather. He used it on Noel once, but never on anyone else that I know of.

Secret: I think Mom didn't approve of it as disciplinary tool. A belt works just fine, thank you.

I painted that bathroom a couple of times. The first time, I painted it Flamingo Pink and Gray, colors that Dad picked out at Posten's Hardware store. A few years later, I thought I'd treat my folks to a nice clean-looking new paint job.

Even though I ordered Flamingo Pink...well, my folks came home to a bright orange bathroom. *Ack!* Fortunately, I only had to cover a quart's worth. After a little thought though, Mom and Dad let it stay bright orange.

• • •

Ever Notice? Department: "Thought" has only one more letter than "though," but they are pronounced differently. How does that work?

• • •

22

The bathroom also included a pretty good-sized walk-in closet. Another favorite hiding place. It was technically Dad's closet, but it also stored the hamper, the vacuum cleaner, a card table, some shotguns and rifles, a canvas rag bag, the shoe-shine box and storage boxes big enough to hide in. The rag bag was where we kept rags. Rags for shining shoes, washing dishes, cleaning up spills, polishing the furniture, scrubbing the bathroom; rags for kite tails, for working out in the tool shed and so forth. It was an excellent place to hide Ruth's girl stuff from her

Even before Noel left home, I had to clean the bathroom every Saturday. The sink, the bathtub, the toilet, mirrors, surfaces and floor. Even the window. I mean, get in there and get down there and scrub!

After I'd been away from home for awhile, it dawned on me why I had to clean the bathroom so much. Because once I overheard Mom tell June Richardson that I cleaned more thoroughly than Ruth. Mom loved me and had a wonderful weekly plan for my life.

But I'd rather clean the bathroom than practice the piano.

For a while the bedroom behind the kitchen/bath was mine and Noel's. We had bunk beds; Noel on top and I on the bottom. Dad slept across from us by the back door. In the other bedroom, a small addition to the house, was Ruth and Mom. As the years rolled by, the two bedrooms got rearranged a half a dozen ways. Neal slept out in "the shed," a room in a shed row out by the alley.

For a couple of years, I slept in the other bedroom. Dad had a bed in there, too, and Mom and Ruth slept in the other room. When Grandmother came once, she and I shared that room.

Eventually, when Neal went off to college, Noel moved out to the shed. When he left for the Army, then I moved out there and Ruth had a whole bedroom all to herself.

On the back wall of the house, blowing directly into my bedroom was a water cooler. No, no, not the kind you drink from, the kind that cooled homes in the hot, dry desert. It was responsible for cooling the whole house. It cooled much better than the heater heated.

On a hot day, after a few hours of hot outdoor fun (or chores), I loved to stand in front of the cooler and let it blow on me. Sometimes I'd toss a little water into it and let it spray back onto me, too. *Mmmm.*

23

That cooler was our best friend. Pick a hot day—any hot day. If we pulled the dark blinds, cracked the kitchen and dining room windows a little, and adjusted the doors just right, we lived in one cool house.

". . . and I will dwell in the house of the Lord forever."

—Psalm 23:6

The Story of Mom's Whistle

Once upon a time there was a brass whistle hanging in the kitchen. It was a sad whistle. It was sad because nobody loved it.

Mom and Dad, who lived there, blew the whistle to call their children home from their playmates' houses. Their children were Paul and Ruth (after their brothers moved away from home). *"Wheeeeeeeet! Wheeeeeeeet!"* the whistle tweeted. Paul and Ruth hated the sound of that brass whistle because it always meant the end of their fun.

The brass whistle tweeted itself loudly enough to be heard clear on the other side of Clawson School. The children had to yell, "Coming!" every time they heard the brass whistle blow. Sometimes it was embarrassing for them to yell "Coming," because their friends teased them.

The brass whistle got excited every time Mom or Dad took it outside to tweet it. *"Wheeeeeeeet! "Wheeeeeeeet!"* it proudly tweeted. It always tweeted as best it knew how, but still the children didn't like it.

Mom or Dad blew that brass whistle at the worst of times. *"Wheeeeeeeet!"* the whistle tweeted, and a great game of baseball or football or marbles or kick-the-can was spoiled. Paul reluctantly said, "Coming!' and sauntered home while his friends kept on having fun. Paul did not like that whistle.

"Ha. Ha. Ha." When Paul's friends got a little older, they worked up the nerve to yell "Coming!" before he did. Not just one boy, all of them—together! "Ha. Ha. Ha," they all laughed. "Yee-haw!" they howled. Mom never did appreciate that.

"Wheeeeeeeet!" "Wheeeeeeeet!" the brass whistle tweeted. "Coming!" Paul yelled. He went home only to find out that Mom or Dad was really calling for Ruth. "But now that you're home…" Mom or Dad said. Then they found some dishes for him to wash or a bathtub to scrub. Those were the times that Paul did not like that whistle at all.

There were a few times, however, when Mom or Dad blew the brass whistle at just the right time. *"Wheeeeeeeet!"* and Paul was rescued from some nervous neighborhood orneriness. "Coming! *Coming!"* He hurried home—even if it meant practicing the piano.

When Paul became a teenager, he got to blow the brass whistle a few times to call Ruth home. Paul never blew that whistle very hard because he knew Ruth didn't like it, either. The brass whistle became sadder and sadder.

One afternoon, when the whistle hadn't blown in several days, Mom took it out on the porch during a big, bad rain storm. Now Mom was terrified of storms and lightning, so she hurried and blew with all her might. *"Wheeee-RRR-EEEEEEEETT!"* the whistle proudly tweeted, better and louder than ever before.

Paul didn't hear it, yet he was only 75 feet away.

Paul was on Patsy Savage's front porch, only two houses over from his, during this awful thunder and lightning storm. It was about four in the afternoon, but it was darker than night. Mean and heavy black clouds were throwing down rain something fierce! Lightning bolts and thunder slashed and clashed all around! The wind blew hard, slinging rain sideways sumptny-dumpum miles an hour!

One angry bolt of lightning exploded right into the middle of street. It didn't just strike. It *strrr-uuu-ck!* With vicious shudders and twists it drilled itself into the pavement. A spooky, shimmering light lit up Seventh Street like noon was having a nightmare. Paul heard the sound of its thunder before its light went out.

In that noisy, brilliant blast of light, for just a couple of seconds, Paul happened to see Mom blowing that proud brass whistle into the storm—but he never heard a bit of it.

Paul wondered why Mom was out on the front porch during a Southern Arizona lightning storm with a brass whistle stuck in her mouth. He never did figure that out. But there she was, wearing a blue-flowered apron.

Paul yelled "Coming!" knowing full well that Mom didn't hear him. He dashed home in that mean, maddening rain. It only took him twelve seconds, but he was drenched through to his bones. Mom wanted him safely in the house. Dry.

26

Many years later, after the brass whistle had proudly tweeted uncounted times, the little family moved to another house. The sad whistle that nobody loved got lost in the shuffle and was never seen—or heard—again.

Paul and Ruth lived happily ever after.

". . . he whistles for those at the ends of the earth.
Here they come, swiftly and speedily!"

—Isaiah 5:26

Wide Streets and Other Playgrounds

For the record, historic old US Highway 80 winds through Douglas on its way from Lordsburg to Benson. It joins I-10 there, but when I lived there it went on to Tucson and points west. Highway 80 used to be the longest highway in America, stretching from Tybee Island, Georgia, to San Diego. Now it stops or starts in Dallas. In Cochise County, old US 80 is now called Arizona 80.

From the northeast, Highway 80 comes in on A Avenue and drifts down to Tenth Street where it passes the First Baptist Church on its way downtown. Then up G Avenue it goes where it bends left at Fifteenth Street, leaves town and goes on to Bisbee. Cars once used an underpass at that intersection, under two sets of train tracks. It was an impressive underpass, too. Well put together. A couple of times it filled with rain water. Only a couple of times. After the railroads stopped stopping in Douglas, the underpass was filled up with dirt and the streets were made level. That underpass is now an attractive and welcoming intersection.

When Mr. Douglas founded Douglas back in the early 1900s, somebody was smart enough to draw straight streets—and wide ones, too. The streets of Douglas are all fairly wide, wide enough for cars to park parallel on both sides and still have plenty of two lane traffic space. The curbs are high, for the most part, which made for great rivulets during and after a good rainfall.

Often—*often!*—we played in the street. We played kick-the-can, four corners, football, baseball. We rode our bikes, of course, and ran foot races. Sometimes we just stood in the middle of the street and talked to each other.

We never played soccer. Or hockey.

At night, bats flew around the street lights where bugs congregated. On summer nights we threw rocks up toward the lights. Sometimes a bat thought it detected some kind of food and flew into the rock at top speed. Oh, what fun that was! Doug's dad, Chet, scolded us if he saw us doing that.

When cars came down the street we had to scoot to one curb or the other till they passed. Douglas traffic is slow. 25 MPH. Traffic is much slower when a bunch of kids are out in it. After dark, it was fun to act like we were stretching a rope across the street. The cars slowed or stopped for us. We laughed and hooted! How sure we were that we'd fooled all those drivers.

After dark, if we were too pooped to play anymore, we sat on the curb till our parents started calling us in.

Sidewalks...

On the sidewalks, which also were rather wide, we skated on skates with metal wheels. There were more bike races and foot races, too.

Those old-fashioned skates had toe clamps at the front, which were adjusted with a skate key, and hard leather straps that fastened around the ankle. They were adjusted lengthwise, by sliding the back end to suit your foot. And if you pulled the two ends completely apart, removed the strap and clamps, nailed the two ends to a two-by-four, then you had a skateboard. I don't think I ever had a new pair of skates, but there was always a pair to be found around the yard. And if you didn't find any in your own yard, why, you just poked around the neighborhood till you found some in another yard. Who cared?

I was a good skater—fast! I never figured out how to skate backward, though.

Lolita Barrett lived across the street at 1123. She couldn't skate. No matter how hard she tried, she never got the hang of it. She was a large girl and was a hoot to watch. She tried and tried. Sort of tip-toeing along, bent well-over, arms waving to keep her balance, her sister laughing at her, she kept on trying until finally...she always gave up at the end of her front fence.

Back to the sidewalks. We played hopscotch, not only on the city sidewalks, but on each other's front walks. Every house had a front walk, except Armando's and the house where John Matson lived. Probably, at any given moment every day of the year, there was a bicycle lying out on the sidewalk somewhere on the block.

Of course, all the silly neighborhood girls had dolls and baby carriages strewn up and down the street.

...Curbs...

The street curbs in Douglas were made for boys. Most were about eight inches high, although some were even higher. First Street, Second Street and Third Street didn't have curbs or sidewalks, though. Most of the residential Avenues (north and south) didn't have curbs, either. I don't know why.

One of the great lazy day pastimes for a Seventh Street boy was throwing a baseball against the curb and fielding it. Maybe it bounced back as a soft fly ball, or came roaring back as a quick grounder. It made for solitary fun and great infield practice. But if you missed and threw it over the top, then there was a trip into the front yard to retrieve it. We learned not to do that too often.

- A little boy learned to balance and walk the curb from corner to corner—but he could never cross the street.

- A brave boy rode his bicycle along the curb, but for only about six feet till he lost his balance, slipped off the curb, collapsed and nearly impaled himself on the handlebars.

- A boy with a baseball stood in the street and played "pitch-back" for hours on end all by himself.

- Aspiring engineers built dams immediately after it rained.

- A couple of boys with Popsicles, watermelon slices or pocket knives sat on the curb and whiled away some idle time.

- Teenage boys painted house numbers on the curb for just fifty cents.

- Teens with new drivers' licenses practiced getting the car really close without touching tires to the curb.

On a quiet evening after dark, those curbs were the most comfortable benches in Douglas, especially with a friend beside you.

...and Alleys

Every block in Douglas has an unpaved alley. All along the alley, from home to home, tall weeds and desert grasses grew. Telephone poles lined the alleys. Each home had some sort of a nook where garbage cans were nestled. The garbage trucks came down the alleys a couple of times a week. Two men riding on steps hopped off and emptied our garbage cans. Then the truck waddled on down to the next couple of cans. There were no dumpsters. There were no trash bags out on the curbs.

Now the alleys were not just a place for garbage trucks. The alley behind our house was a familiar to me as Our Back Yard. In a way, it was another extension of the yard. Many back yards had wide gates for cars to enter. Ours did, and Dad often parked the pickup back there. Certainly he did when it was time to load or unload beehives. But he also parked back there to load or unload junk, change the oil or fix a flat tire.

Alleys were a short cut to somewhere else. Almost every time we walked somewhere besides Seventh Street, we left via the alley. We played lots of games in the alleys, too. Usually, bike races or hide and seek. There were no hidden treasures in the alleys; there were too many kids in the neighborhood to let anything "valuable" stay for long. The alleys were not a place for solitary fun. In an alley you always had to have a buddy with you. Richie Verdugo's family lived across the alley from us, on Eighth Street, so it was common to easily slip over there for fun and games on Eighth Street.

"The chariots storm through the streets, rushing back and forth through the squares. They look like flaming torches; they dart about like lightning."

—Nahum 2:4

Fight! Fight!

And oh, yes. Alleys were the place where school boys settled their differences. Every once in awhile a couple of boys duked it out pretty good in some Douglas alley, not far from a school yard. They always attracted quite a crowd, too.

I got into an alley "fight" with Stephen Whitehead once up by the Junior High School. We were friends, too, for cryin' out loud. I suppose we circled each other and swung at the air for fifteen minutes. We managed to get our clothes torn and dirty from wrestling around. Our Seventh Grade music teacher, whose name I forgot, stood by his fence and watched. Steve and I had such a non-fight, that he didn't even try to break us up like a respectable adult was supposed to.

Tommy Jay beat me up in an alley another time. Again Junior High. Tommy is a lot bigger than I. A funny thing happened: no matter how hard I tried, I couldn't bring myself to swing at him. I wanted to. In fact, I wound up and cocked a magnificent right cross. He saw it coming and froze in fear. I froze, too. I couldn't throw it, and I'll never know why. Had I hit him, he'd still be reeling. All I did that day was futilely fend off what he threw at me—and took a pounding.

A Mexican boy rescued me. He walked up to Tommy and knocked him to his knees with one powerful punch to the stomach. Tommy and I never said much to each other after that.

When we lived at 1123, several boys were beating the tar out of Noel in the alley behind Mrs. Jackson's house (two houses over). Clawson School had just let out and a horde of boys and girls were really giving it to Noel. But our Super Dad went to his rescue! Super Dad charged out the front door (not the back door) to teach that gang of fourth grade thugs a lesson they'd never forget! He got in the car and...

"Daddy, can I go, too?" I yelled from the porch steps.

"Alright. Hurry up and get in," he said.

He waited for me. All the while Noel was getting the tar beat out of him. When I was safely in, Dad maneuvered a U-turn in the street. From A Avenue he drove into the alley—but first he smacked the telephone pole and ruined the right fender. Ooh! That made him mad! He scrambled out and wrenched the fender away from the tire. All the while Noel was getting the tar beat out of him. Dad backed up and pointed straight down the alley. He zoomed up the alley about fifteen miles an hour and came to a dusty, crunching halt in front of that pack of Fourth Grade outlaws who were beating the tar out of his son. "Stay in the car!" he barked at me. No problem!

Noel was or had been crying. He had a bloody nose and was all sweaty. Dad jumped out but the hooligans kept right on beating the tar out Noel. Dad didn't say a word. He spied a two-by-four with a bunch of jagged, rusty nails all over it.

When he picked it up and headed for the crowd, the crowd was no more. Off everyone ran in every direction, leaving Noel alone in the middle of the alley crying. When he got in the car Super Dad drove in reverse back to A Avenue. Why reverse? Because he left that nail-laden two-by-four in front of the car and was too angry to get out and toss it to one side.

I was about four at that time, and Noel must have been in the fourth grade. I have no knowledge (or memory) of any conversation that immediately followed that after-school beating. Poor Noel.

Today's test: Explain why Super Dad got in the car and drove around to the alley to confront those boys who were beating the tar out of his son? Why didn't he bound over the fence and attack them? Why did he wait patiently for me to get in the car, too? How much damage did he do to the fender? (Answer: Quite a bit, but he never had the extra cash to fix it, so it stayed bent for five or six more years.)

"I will fight no more forever."

—Chief Joseph, Nez Perce Indian Tribe

Vacant Lots

The 1100 block of Seventh Street had three vacant lots for many years. There were also three houses set all the way back against the alley, creating three additional lots out by the sidewalk. The lot between the Barrett's house and Mrs. Jackson's house was the biggest, so we used it the most. The other two lots were on the corners at A Avenue and at Bonita Avenue. Those lots didn't get as much attention, but they can tell some tales, too. There was also a vacant lot behind us on Eighth Street between Richie Verdugo's house and George and Eva Hatt's.

In these lots we played with our toy trucks and cars and flew kites. Noel flew a neat box kite once that he kept up for *hours*.

We dug holes half way to China, hoping to find some buried treasure. We never discovered any, so we filled those holes and dug 'em again next year.

We built several forts of dirt, sticks, old boards, cardboard boxes and ocotillo branches. We played cowboys and Indians with shiny new cap pistols and hand-made bows and arrows. We argued a lot, shared Pepsi Colas and Popsicles, had rock fights and mud fights. We punted footballs and shagged pop flies, shot marbles, staged Olympic track meets and conducted warfare.

We sucked the sweet nectar of ocotillo blossoms and ate pomegranates under the shady branches of a big mesquite tree.

Sometimes we just played hop-scotch.

We played marbles in the lots a lot, usually in front of Armando's house. We always played for keeps. At best, I was a really mediocre marble shooter. Frequently some of my allowance went for more new marbles. Armando was the best and always brought the most marbles, which he kept in old canvas money sacks. About three bags full. Everyone's goal was to get his "shooter." It was intimidating and as clear as any marble ever made. No one ever got it. We were convinced that his shooter was the secret of his great success. That he was skillful never entered our minds.

Each lot had at least one yucca cactus in it. The Lord put them there long before Douglas was founded. Yuccas have long needles (or leaves), each one almost two feet long. They spike out in every direction of the compass. The porcupines of cacti. They're hardy, patient plants, making the most of the little bit of desert water that falls their way. Some kinds of yuccas produce pretty white flowers every year; other only occasionally, and a few just once every 100 years. Normally, people (and desert animals) don't mess with yuccas.

I was about 12 when I won a football in a Cochise County Fair pet contest. (I took a queen bee, much to the delight of my dad.) It was the first prize I ever won! It was new and beautiful! I held on tight, not daring to drop it or get it dirty. That "new" leather smell filled the car all the way home where I proudly showed Mom. Dad was proud, too.

"Well, that's a nice one," Mom said. "Now you take good care of it."

"I'm going to!" I assured her.

Was there ever a boy more proud of a new football? I dashed out of the house to show my friends. But first I took it to the lot across the street and kicked it as hard and as high as I ever kicked anything. Really high! Way higher than Butchie Barrett's house.

It rocketed down right into the heart of one of those yuccas. That ball went into that cactus with such force that the needles were driven all the way through it. There must have been 200 holes in that ball. I took care of it, all right.

In a flash it was flattened—and I'm still crushed.

"...and He will wipe away every tear..."

—Revelation 21:4

Noel and Mr. Whitemule

My brother Noel once brought home a pure white mule. Rumor has it he found it in Mexico. I don't know where he got it. He never confessed to anything but "...out in the desert."

It was a good-looking mule. Big, tall, wide and wild. He looked awfully self-confident. He had a proud stance that said, "I'm in charge!"

Had it ever been ridden? None of us were brave enough to find out.

Noel brought it home because he wanted to lead it along in a parade, which was scheduled just a day or two away. A handsome white mule in a small town parade? Why not?

Well, he didn't quite get the mule all the way home. In the vacant lot across the street, right at the edge of the sidewalk, Mr. Whitemule stopped. He stopped for good. Noel pulled on the rope. No luck. Stretched his neck out pretty good. No luck. Noel pounded on Mr. Whitemule's dusty flanks. Nope. Didn't work. Noel yelled. Whipped. Pulled some more.

A crowd of neighborhood boys—some girls, too—gathered round to watch and cheer. "Do this, Noel. Do that, Noel." "Come on, Mule!"

A couple of moms stood on their porches admonishing, "You boys be careful!"

Noel sent me into the house for a carrot. Mr. Whitemule turned his nose up at it. We tried again with a whole bunch of carrots. Mr. Whitemule wasn't hungry. Noel got a friend to help him pull. Billy Duncan tried to push. Mr. Whitemule's feet were firmly planted, his head held high, his ears standing tall, his big ol' eyeballs rolling around watching Noel's every move.

Then Dad came home from work. He came over to watch. He had two questions: "Where'd you get him?" and "How long's he been here?"

"About an hour," Noel replied.

Dad walked back to the house, changed his clothes and came back. He slapped Mr. Whitemule around a little. Mr. Whitemule just stood there unimpressed. Dad said, "Well, if he decides to let go, bring him into the back yard." With that he walked away.

Noel and all the rest of us started over again. Yelling, pulling, whipping, smacking, pushing on Mr. Whitemule. He was a stubborn old mule.

About thirty minutes later Dad returned carrying an eight-foot long crowbar. One end was glowing red hot. Even in the bright sunlight, that thing glowed. The crowd backed away. Way away. Dad showed the bar to the mule, even held it up close to his nose, but Mr. Whitemule was a stubborn old mule.

Can you believe this? Dad put a four inch brand on the back of that stubborn old mule and he still wouldn't move!

Dad got behind Mr. Whitemule and jammed that crowbar where the sun don't shine. Mr. Whitemule wasn't stubborn anymore. He kicked up both hind legs, just missing Dad, who was smart enough to get an eight-foot bar. Dad poked him once more for good measure. Mr. Whitemule danced a quick little mule dance. Noel triumphantly led him to our back yard.

That night, we peeked out our bedroom window to see Mr. Whitemule glowing in the moonlight. He marched in the parade a couple of days later and then Noel released him back into Mexico...er, I mean, the desert.

"Do not be like the horse or the mule..."

—Psalm 32:9

The Neatest Driveway on Earth

Do you know how many stars are in the desert sky?

- Count the baseballs I pitched down our driveway.

- Count the honeysuckle blossoms I sucked from the shady vine that grew against our west wall.

- Count the hide and seek and kick-the-can games that involved our driveway.

- Count the foot races from the sidewalk to the garage door.

- Count the times I climbed one of those tall shady tamarisk trees that lined our driveway.

- Tell me how many times Dad tinkered on his pickup.

- Tell me how many times Mom got the car stuck in the driveway.

- Tell me how many beehives we unloaded in front of the garage.

- Tell me how many miles our family walked up and down that driveway over the years.

Add them all up and then you'll know how many stars are in a desert sky.

Character. That's what our driveway had. No other driveway on the block—or even in Douglas—was as cool as ours. Mrs. Savage's was just as long, but it was paved and sterile, and no respectable kid would touch it.

Our driveway beamed proudly when four cars somehow got lined up in it. It welcomed neighbors and visitors of every stripe. It was eager to provide plenty of shade on the hottest August day. It was happy when children's laughter ran up and down it. It was a haven for bikes, wagons, doll strollers and motor scooters. It was a hideout for lazy cats and dogs.

It was strewn with taped-up baseballs, chipped 7-Up bottles, rusty rakes and shovels, broken baseball bats, bent buckets, ruined inner tubes and all kinds of other wonderful treasures.

You had to really work hard to get in trouble in our driveway, or even get scolded. It was just too cool for orneriness.

It was a natural playground that stretched about 70 feet or so from the front sidewalk, along the west side of the house, and on to the garage, which sat about 20 feet past the house. It wasn't paved, nor was the inside of the garage. Dirt, shade, trees to climb, branches to swing from, a couple of low fences and one high fence, secret hiding places—perfect for boys.

I was eight when I realized I'd someday pitch for the NY Yankees. I hung an old tire on the garage door and paced off the right distance to my pitcher's mound. My pitching rubber was usually an old board or a flattened tin can. Or I just dug a line with the heel of my shoe. Then I set about throwing balls and strikes. Not that many strikes, though, which was frustrating.

The only problem I had was retrieving each pitch. Unless I convinced my sister to shag my pitches and toss them back to me, I had to go get every pitch and return to the mound. I'll bet Whitey Ford or Duke Snyder or Sandy Koufax never had to shag their own pitches.

Once in a while, I played catch with someone my size and age. We took turns pitching. We pitched till we struck out three or until we walked in one run. Then we switched positions. The catcher was also the umpire. Baseball is too sacred for us to cheat. We called 'em like we saw 'em. Once Doug Foster and I "played" a whole game. I think he won, something like 6 to 3.

A wonderfully thick honeysuckle vine grew twelve feet high next to our house, keeping the west side of the house a little cooler.

My all-time favorite thing to do in the driveway was to sit in the shade between the house and the honeysuckle trellis. Especially when it was full of blossoms and bees. Yum-yum!

When Leonard Heuberger and I still played with little trucks and cars, we drove them many a mile in that narrow space. I read my comic books there. I tried my hand at whittling with a pocket knife (but never got too far). Home-made popsicle cubes, frozen in the ice tray, were extra tasty back there. For a long while that was my personal place of refuge. When my feelings got hurt, that's where I pouted.

If we had to retrieve my sister's doll from the roof, the trellis was our ladder up there.

One important kick-the-can rule for the driveway was "…you can't touch the can with your hands." So naturally, we always kicked it into the trellis or in the tall grass between a couple of trees. That way we had a little more time to hide while whoever was "it" was fishing out the can with his feet. The Neatest Driveway on Earth was the only place we used that rule.

Armando Contreras hated to be "it." He cheated any way possible to get someone else "it," including picking up the can with his hands and running it back.

The driveway was a dangerous place when Mom was driving. Stay to one side and keep your eye on her.

"Next to my citizenship, I consider my driver's license the greatest privilege I have," I once heard Mom tell a friend.

I was about ten when she got her first driver's license. How, I don't know: she couldn't drive any better than a frog. Going forward was easy for her; backing up was impossible.

Often, Dad parked the car in the garage before he went to work. If Mom needed the car, she always tried to back out. That meant backing up seventy feet or so to the street. For some bizarre reason, she only made it about twenty feet right into a tamarisk tree. She pulled forward and tried again. Then she bumped into the honeysuckle trellis on the other side of the driveway. She kept trying, though.

"Stop, Mom!" She almost hit the house.

After four or five short maneuvers, each one ending in her own personal one-car traffic jam, she gave up and asked Mr. Kaine next door to get her out of her fix. Mr. Kaine effortlessly moved the car out onto the street, pointed in the right direction.

Mom was always grateful to him for that—and relieved. Off she'd go. Oh, so slowly. Give her credit, though. She learned to drive with a clutch and a floor shift. I always considered it some sort of a miracle that she ever learned to drive at all. She was so short. Hidden down behind the steering wheel, it took great effort for her to peer over the dashboard.

Mom, why didn't you just ask Mr. Kaine in the first place? And Dad, why didn't you ever put the car in the street before you went to work?

Well, he did—eventually. In 1958 he bought a '53 Buick. That was one boat of a car, I tell you. It was three times bigger than the '37 Chevy we had and the gear shifter was in the steering column. Mom had to learn to drive all over again—and it was harder for her to see over the dashboard.

But she did learn to ask before Dad went to work. "Daddy?" (That's what she called him in front of us.) "Will you pull the car out for me?"

Good grief, Dad. What a simple solution!

"The boundary lines have fallen for me in pleasant places; surely I have a delightful inheritance."

—Psalm 16:6

41

Friend of the Bees, Part 1

Bees are an integral part of my life.

I've been told that Dad was out buying a hive of bees the night I was born. Maybe that's why I'm so sweet. He was a well respected beekeeper, renown in the industry, beloved in the community. He loved his bees like he loved his children, and he loved to teach others his hobby. My dad was a friend of the bees and there were times I admired how he worked among them unprotected.

We had beehives in Our Back Yard every day that we lived at 1122. They were as much a part of the yard as the fence and the dirt. There were usually three to six hives. Out at Slaughter's Ranch Dad kept dozens. Dozens!

Although Dad sold his honey, it never bothered him to give away honey by the case. You might say he was running a "non-profit organization." It bothered Mom, though. Almost everyone who visited our home went home with a jar of honey. Out-of-town relatives got a whole case.

"Aren't you afraid of getting stung?" was a common question. No, I wasn't. Dad taught us early on not to swat at bees when they were close at hand. I only got stung once.

Rudy Campos had just moved into the neighborhood and wanted to see the inside of a beehive. One evening about sunset I dressed him up in one of dad's protective hats. He put on a coat even though it was pretty warm. He wanted even more protection, so we found a large piece of dirty carpet and wrapped him in that, too. ('Fraidy-cat.)

Usually there were two protective hats (veils) around, but not this time. So I decided to open the hive without one. Hey, my dad does it all the time and no bees ever sting him. Why can't I?

I got a pry bar and carefully pried the top off. Not carefully enough. It popped and bounced a little and... *Blapp! Blapp-edy-blapp-blapp!* Those ornery bees pounced all over my face and all through my hair!

"Ouch! Ouch! Ouch!" I never saw bees come out of a hive that fast! I dropped the top down—loudly and horribly crooked. More bees. My pry bar went flying somewhere and those bees came after me like bees after honey. Yes, I've been stung! All over my face and scalp with some on my shoulder to boot. *"Sting! Stang! Stung!*

Rudy made a beeline for his house and I made a beeline out the back gate. Up the alley I flew, all the while blindly flailing away at my attackers. Thankfully, up around the Foster's house they decided they had chased me far enough. I circled the block and cautiously walked back home—through the front door.

At that time Dad was working the swing shift and Mom and Ruth were over at the Richardson's house. I walked five blocks to their house for some sympathy. By the time I got there I had puffed up really good. My face looked like a sack of golf balls.

When I went in Mom squealed a little when she saw me. June Richardson said, "What have you got yourself into this time?" They counted twenty-three stings.

Rudy escaped unscathed.

The next morning, after Dad heard about it, he told me, "That was the meanest swarm of bees I ever saw. You should have opened a different hive."

How was I to know he'd just captured a wild swarm? How was I to know he had just put them into that hive to settle down? How was I to know that they hadn't settled down yet?

Rudy Campos never set foot in Our Back Yard again.

"They surrounded me, yes, they surrounded me…they surrounded me like bees…"

—Psalm 118:11, 12

Friend of the Bees, Part 2

Are bees like dogs? You know, dogs are part of your family. They'd never bite any of you. Well, unless you're pulling on its ears like Ruth used to do. But then you'd only get nipped. So, do backyard bees leave you alone, but sting intruding neighbors? Except for the time I was mauled by that angry swarm, I've never been stung. No, never. And I've been among lots of bees.

Dad's been stung a number of times. I've seen his eyes nearly swollen shut a couple of times, but he never complained. He always said, "I should have known better."

There were many times when he went out to the backyard, got himself a little bee and made her sting him on the shoulder. Then his arthritis pain went away for a few weeks. He really didn't like sacrificing her, but...

I'm convinced that bees, like family pets, know who takes care of them. So they don't sting people in that family. I'm also convinced that Dad was a friend of the bees and communicated with them, much like good dog owners communicate with their dogs.

I've walked among bees in our back yard. On spring mornings I've sat close to their hives and watched them go sailing in and out. I've inserted winter feed into their hives. I've opened hives, smoked the bees and brushed them off heavy frames of honey comb. I've stood among curious bees for hours, helping Dad extract honey. I squatted in front of their hives and watched as they took turns "air conditioning" the hive. Sometimes I did these things without protection. All the while, bees buzzed around me, taking a look to see if I was sweet enough to carry into the hive. Some landed on me and wandered around. Most just buzzed by to say "hello."

On a spring morning, they filled our honeysuckle trellis with muzzic. Out at Slaughter's ranch they frolicked among all the bright yellow mesquite trumpets. I've taken close-up photos of ecstatic bees nuzzling up to fresh spring blossoms. The bees and I drank water together from the artesian pond on Slaughter's Ranch. Oh, and did you know that bees dance? Yes, bees dance. They do! They're lovely little creatures who make our honey—one of God's great treats.

•   •   •

Ever Notice? Department: The last four letters of "great" and "treat" are the same but pronounced differently. How does that work?

•   •   •

Some time after the Rudy Campos incident, I decided to open another hive without protection (but in a long sleeved shirt). I was sure it really is possible to open up a hive without getting stung. It was a cool afternoon that day, maybe autumn, probably Saturday. Aware that I might get stung up again, I went in among the bees anyway. Only a few were out. I was careful and quiet as I inserted the pry bar and lifted.

If they didn't sting me, I'd be a friend of the bees, and my "pet" theory would be right.

The top came off almost silently. The busy bees kept on working in there. I spoke to them. "Hi. I'm just looking," I said. "It's alright." A few came out to see me, the others ignored me. I gently replaced the top over my friends. With a deep satisfactory breath I tenderly placed one hand on the top, then walked away. "I guess I'm gonna be like my dad," I said to myself. "I'm gonna be a friend of the bees."

That is my secret. And that was not the only time I safely opened a hive of bees without protection.

"Satisfy us in the morning with your unfailing love, that we may sing for joy and be glad all our days."

—Psalm 90:14

45

Slaughter's Ranch

Dad kept the majority of his beehives on John Slaughter's Ranch. Tall hives, short hives, long rows of hives, hives scattered around. For a brief time, while we three boys were all at home to help, Dad had a little more than 200 beehives. At the time, more than anyone else in Arizona.

His hives stood just outside an enormous grove of mesquite bushes. They're not the same as the wannabe mesquites found in Texas. In Southern Arizona those mesquite bushes produce lots of luscious yellow trumpet flowers. Perfect for bees and perfect for the clearest, most golden honey you ever saw. Tastiest, too. To this day, I've not eaten honey as good as my dad's.

Just a few of Dad's beehives. The adults are my first cousins, Bob and Elsie Mae Bayles. They were unafraid of the bees because it was a cold winter day. The bees were hunkered down. Smart bees.

When he had the opportunity, Dad took friend and foe alike out to Slaughter's to show off his impressive rows of bees: "Nichols Honey Rock Apiary." Psalm 81:16 says "…with honey from the rock I will satisfy you." Dad's apiary is named from that verse.

Dad's honey jar label. Courtesy of my sister, Ruth.

Anyway, Slaughter's was a great place for any boy growing up in Southern Arizona. A kid could shoot to his heart's content, whether he hit anything or not.

Out there on Slaughter's Ranch, I saw my only puma bounding along just like you see on TV. Rabbits galore. Coyotes, buzzards, hawks by the ka-zillion. Awful skunks, too. Ducks in Mr. Slaughter's pond, snakes—oh yes, diamondbacks! Dad killed a couple. In my day there were fenced-in cattle, a few lazy horses and a couple of lazier donkeys.

The ranch house is made of stone about twelve inches thick. The floor is also stone. It was always cool inside. I took a few naps in there. (On the Internet I found a picture of John Slaughter and his wife standing near the front door of that house. I've stood there, too.)

About a mile past the ranch house, down another narrow, one lane, dusty, bumpy road, was a working bottle house. That's where artesian water was bottled for sale. Just beyond was a natural, free-flowing water fountain.

From out of the ground and through an eight-inch pipe came the best tasting water I ever swallowed. I straddled the pipe and stuck my face right into the flowing water. I drank my fill and refilled my

47

canteen. That's one way I cooled off out there. A long, thick string of emerald green moss hung from the end of the pipe. I liked to squeeze its softness.

The water fell into a pool full of pond lilies and dragon flies. Bees, butterflies and other flying friends stopped by, too. There were always animal tracks along the edges. Local desert animals (not the cattle) stopped by to refresh themselves, too. I never saw any, I only saw the tracks they left behind. Dad took empty glass milk jugs out there and brought them home full of good drinking water.

Sometimes I just sat on the pipe and listened to the water spill into the pond. It's steady, dreamy splash was the only sound...

I loved to walk around alone out at Slaughters. Many times I left Dad to his bees and wandered off to find us some supper. I took home a few dead rabbits now and then. I always made a pilgrimage to the artesian water pond.

About every thirty minutes I fired off a shot in the general direction of the bees just to let Dad know I was doing okay. I usually ate my sandwich under a shady tree near the cow pasture.

Dad always "mmeep-mmeeped" when it was time for me to return to the dusty road. When we met up he always—yes, always—had full water jugs and a big bunch of fresh water cress he'd pulled from the pond. We usually rode home silently. Sometimes I got to drive.

Dad wouldn't let me invite my friends to go out there. Not because of the bees, but because we were out in the stillness of the hot desert; out where no one heard us or saw us. Out where the sky is big and the noonday sun never moves. Out where breezes are forbidden; where heat wins every argument. Out where the rocky ground is sharp and hot. Out where the spirit of the great Apaches follows you along the desert floor. Out where water is only a mirage and shade comes only at night. Out where everything is about a hundred miles from here.

Ah, the Southern Arizona desert. What a great place. *What a special place!* Especially when your dad is close by.

Dad took a few of Neal and Noel's friends out there one day. I rode in the front of the pickup with Dad. All the other lucky boys got to ride in the back. I was five or six years old, I guess, on a screaming hot summer day. We let Dad go to work with his bees, enthusiastically took off through the mesquite grove and promptly got lost in the desert...

We Were Out Where the Sky is Big

We were out where the sky is big and the noonday sun never moves.

Not to worry. Those 12- and 13-year-old boys knew how to wander through the desert. "You always go to the right," one of them suggested.

"No you don't. You go to the left, that way."

"My dad said always go uphill."

"Well, your dad ain't here and its five miles to the nearest hill. We're going right, okay?"

"Always go downhill is what my dad said."

Along the way we went through a grove of cottonwood trees. For some reason, those bigger boys refused to turn around and go back through them. I thought going back where we came from was the best idea, but I was the youngest and the littlest, so they ignored me altogether.

We shuffled into a dry, sandy creek bed and found a shady spot under a big tree. Everyone but Neal and me got naked and buried themselves in the sand. They needed to, too, because (I learned later) they were all over-exposed to the sun. They weren't being naughty, they were cooling off because we were out where heat settles all arguments; where breezes are forbidden.

About this time, everyone took turns hollering for Dad.

"Hello! Hello!"

"Dad. Hello?"

"Hey! Hey! Hello-oh!"

"Dad-dee!"

But we were out in the stillness of the hot desert; out where no one heard us or saw us.

I kept saying to Neal, "Let's go back through those trees." But—and who knows why—he kept saying, "We can't." So I kept on worrying.

Evening was approaching. We were all hollering at once now. And walking! Walking and walking out where the rocky ground is sharp and hot and everything is about a hundred miles from here. Where we were walking to I don't know, but the sun was behind us,

I detected concern in Neal. Uh-oh. Suddenly I was nervous. I was hungry, too. *"Mom,"* I whimpered quietly. Was I scared? I don't think so, but you have to remember: I was with my big brothers.

Noel was sure "we have to go this way." His friends were sure "we have to go that way." I'm sure we had no idea where we were, except in Southern Arizona where the spirit of the great Apaches follows you along the desert floor.

Bicker, bicker, bicker.

Holler, holler, *holler!*

Then someone said, "Hey, I think I heard something!"

"What was it? What direction? What'd it sound like?"

"Shut up! Listen!"

From a distance we heard "Mmeep. Mmeep." That sound didn't belong in the desert. It was Dad's pickup horn! We really hollered then!

Like bees attracted to honey, the hollering and the "mmeeping" soon came together. Dad's face was hard and stern when he found us. He had artesian water for everyone, served up from one-pound coffee cans. I was so tired that I slept all the way back home.

That was the only time I was lost out at Slaughters. That's why Dad wouldn't let me invite my friends out there. My big brothers are to blame. I would have gone back through that grove of cottonwoods.

Did Neal and Noel get in trouble? I don't know, but I do know that Noel glowed bright pink for a couple of days.

"…I once was lost, but now am found…"

—from Amazing Grace by John Newton

In Our Back Yard We Recycled

One thing I like about my family: we never threw anything away. There were three rules-of-thumb about things no longer useful.

1. For anything broken: "Hmm. This might come in handy someday." Put it in a pile somewhere.

2. For magazines and literature: "[*Insert name here*] will love this article. And there's a recipe in there that..." Put it in a stack somewhere.

3. For excess new things, like towels and such: "We'll put this in Ruth's hope chest." However, Ruth will tell you there wasn't much excess.

We recycled. We didn't call it that and nobody carted it off in a blue plastic bin. Newspapers were stuffed among honey jars, lined the garbage can and padded packages. Coffee cans held rusty nails according to size. Granger pipe tobacco cans is where we tossed oily nuts and bolts. Metal Band-Aid cans were perfect for Dad's stick matches, which he stashed all over the place. Table scraps either fed the dog and chickens or got buried in the garden. Not a shirt we ever owned went anywhere but into the rag bag.

Mason jars were used for pet lizards and horned toads. Oh, yes, for canning apricots, too. Not to mention the rusty pocket knives, second-hand razor blades, a couple of tarnished army belt buckles and important things like that. Mason jars also kept lots of little car engine parts that might come in handy one of these days.

Wax-coated, cardboard milk cartons (the quart size) were cut into thirds to start new tomato plants. The tops and bottoms were also saved to get a roaring fire going in Dad's burn barrel. Was something made of wood? Into the lumber pile.

We had a general junk box out in the tool shed. Clock parts, extra thermometers, partial coils of wire, burnt out radio tubes, handles and knobs of every sort, bicycle parts, some copper folk art that Aunt

Crosie lovingly made for us, little scales and compasses that didn't work, half a dozen hammer heads, long strands of electric cord yanked out of busted lamps, big bolts, wads of string, one binoculars lens, home-made metal signs, bent aluminum drinking glasses, worthless flashlight batteries, useless flashlights, ancient license plates, stubby pencils with no erasers, a couple of wobbly picture frames—you get the picture.

That junk box itself was a piece of junk. It was green; well-seasoned. Stenciled and faded on both sides was "Apache Powder Company, Benson, Arizona." It originally held dynamite. Over time, we pounded several nails into it to keep it together.

Speaking of old junk boxes; peaches and oranges were shipped to market in wooden crates. As far as Dad was concerned, they were valuable crates for a number of uses—especially useful for tossing things into. We carted beekeeping odds and ends, spare parts, extra tools and so forth. The crates came with colorful and creative paper labels on one end. So when one of those crates started to break down, Dad had us knock all the slats off and pull all the nails out. The wood went into the lumber pile; the end with the label was saved. Dad thought they were pretty. And they were. But they weren't cared for and eventually they disappeared. Those labels will fetch a pretty penny nowadays—if someone can find them.

Hey! We had at least thirty baby food jars filled with screws and washers and little brass springs. My folks recycled before there ever was such a word. My folks knew they'd come in handy someday.

See that old wash tub over there? The one filled with all that scrap metal? There's a sink trap with a hole in it. That might be good for something someday. Flat, twisted copper tubing. Hmmm. Look at all those pieces of metal with sharp, piercing points. What's that old water hose doing tangled up in there? Must have forty pieces of tape wrapped around it. Aw, a bent bumper jack. Dull, worn out shovel blades. I wonder where these horseshoes came from? Twisted, wadded chicken wire. Flattened tin cans. Hey, we can sail 'em across the street!

We boys were welcome to any piece of junk we wanted, no matter how dangerous. If it stayed in the tub for more than a year, though,

Dad made a bittersweet trip to the junk yard and sold it for a little cash—but always brought home the tub.

For an eighth grade science project I made a hygrometer to measure the relative humidity. First, I nailed two small thermometers to a dirty board...

I got an A on my project, never paid a nickel for it and never left Our Back Yard to make it. The stuff really did come in handy. Dad was so proud.

"Their land is full...there is no end to their treasures."

—Isaiah 2:7

Neatly Stacked Lumber in Our Back Yard

Dad was always on the lookout for discarded boards. Every once in awhile he'd come home with a load of scrap lumber he located somewhere in town.

There were two reasons he snapped it up. One was to give it to Mexican people across the line so they'd have cooking and heating fuel. The other reason was because "I might be able to use this someday."

Any boards that remotely resembled "good," went into our lumber pile. The rest he took to a family or two in Agua Prieta.

Oh, no, no! If a board is full of bent rusty nails, pull them out and put them in the bent rusty nail can with all the others. They'll come in handy someday.

Neal and Dad made me a pair of sturdy stilts one time with boards that came in handy that day. They lasted several years and tromped quite a few times up and down the Neatest Driveway on Earth.

From that lumber pile came two permanent tree houses, a few temporary clubhouses and plenty of forts. Dad used a lot of those second-hand boards for his beehives.

He used a whole lot of them for roaring fires under the burn barrel. That was always fun.

We boys (and girls) were welcome to all the wood we wanted. I made all kinds of whatchamacallits. We sawed and hammered two dozen "forts." If we didn't like the looks of one, why, we just knocked it down and made another one. We made forts and hideouts in Our Back Yard, in the vacant lots and down the street in "the desert." The worst part of making them outside the yard was hauling the boards back home when we finished. We were not allowed to leave them behind because "...they might come in handy someday."

We moved the lumber pile several times. Maybe to make way for a chicken pen. Or a pigeon coop. Perhaps Dad needed room to stack more beehive supers (a section of a beehive). Who knows? It was okay because there is nothing quite like a long piece of lumber in your hands. Just carrying it around is one of life's most pleasant chores.

About once a month, we whittled down the wood pile by loading the pickup and delivering scrap wood to Pastor Ybarra over across the line. He was the only Baptist minister in Agua Prieta and one of Dad's best friends. His family cooked and heated with the wood.

Perhaps someday Neal will show you a nifty paddle he made out in Our Back Yard. He came home from college one long weekend, apparently just to make that paddle. The business end of it was shaped like the United States. He patiently cut it out with a coping saw. He carefully sanded, stained and varnished it, and finally decorated it with his fraternity letters. With its long handle, it had a guitar look to it.

I thought it was pretty neat. He must have thought it was pretty neat, too, because he still has it in his home after all these years.

"Whatever your hand finds to do, do it with all your might…"

—Ecclesiastes 9:10

Famous Tree Houses in Our Back Yard

It's true: "If you build it, they will come." We had the favorite back yard in the neighborhood. We had two tree houses.

Next to the garage grew a tall, shady chinaberry tree. Across the yard by the Mason's fence was an even shadier apricot tree. What do you think that boys with plenty of boards and hammers and bent nails would do with trees like that?

First, Noel built a tree house in the chinaberry tree. Sawing and hammering up in a tree looked like an awful lot of fun. But I guess Dad thought I was too little then, or maybe Noel didn't want me in his tree house. They only let me watch from the ground. George Kaine helped, though, and Neal may have, too.

Noel's tree house was a perfect cube. I have no idea of what secret plans to conquer the world were concocted up there. I do know that Noel and his friends read comic books by the score up there. I saw George heft a box of comics up there one day. He held the neighborhood record for the biggest comic book collection— boxes and boxes of them.

A few years later I built a tree house in our apricot tree. Dad gave me a coffee can full of rusty nails and some fantastic tongue-in-groove flooring he had found. I had a delightfully smooth floor in my tree house—except where I bent some nails.

It was long and narrow with a low roof—like a refrigerator box laid on its side. It was a good house and a sturdy one despite the fact that I used boards of every size and color for the walls. I installed a working door and a paneless window, which I used for spying on Seventh Street. I liked my tree house. Quite frankly, it was ugly—but not to me.

Every neighborhood boy climbed up there with me lots of times. About four boys fit in there comfortably. Just for the fun of it our moms packed us lunches once in awhile and we ate up there. We stood on the roof, picked apricots and ate as many as we wanted. We read comic books up there, too, and traded baseball cards.

When the apricots were ripe, hungry boys visited Our Back Yard quite often. They were big and tasty and juicy. One summer the tree was loaded. Loaded, I tell you. We gave away several sacks of apricots to our friends and left plenty for the birds.

One morning that year Doug Foster and I filled a three-gallon pail with apricots, eating as we picked. We picked under the tree house, on top of it, all around it. We didn't even dent the number of apricots. The tree was loaded, I tell you. He lugged them home, and I waddled into the house, too full to eat lunch.

About supper time, Doug came back with that three-gallon pail, but now it was full of plums, cherries and a few peaches—fresh-picked from the Foster's back yard.

"My mom said to give these to you," he told my mom. "It's a trade for the apricots." I explained to Mom. She seemed grateful, and we had plums and cherries for a long time. Doug had the runs.

My tree house was a natural hiding place during hide-and-seek games. Of course, that was the first place whoever was "it" looked. It was a hideout when we played cops and robbers and a spy's nest in times of war. Whenever we had visitors, any kids that came along got taken directly to my tree house.

Doug and I rode out a pretty good rain storm up there once. Stayed dry, too. When the rain stopped, we climbed down, shaking the wet leaves as we went. We might as well have stayed in the rain.

No girls allowed! But I found evidence that Ruth and her friends found their way up there when I wasn't home.

I enjoyed the solitude of it, and on a few boring Saturday evenings read my Sunday School lesson up there. I spent a few summer nights up there, too. I hauled some bedding up there, took comic books and a flashlight, and soon fell asleep in my clothes.

It's pretty neat to wake up in a tree house that you built yourself.

"In my Father's house are many rooms. . .I am going there to prepare a place for you."

—Jesus, John 14:2

A Big "X" Marks the Spot in Our Back Yard

I was eleven when I fell out of the chinaberry tree. My Sunday School friend David Coffey came over after swimming lessons and we went up into Noel's tree house. On the way down, I placed my foot on a bucket that was placed upside down on the picket fence. The bucket moved. Oops! I dangled by one hand for a moment, then fell onto the fence. One picket gored me and ripped a gash behind my shoulder joint.

"Paul! You're bleeding!" David screamed from a branch. Instantly, blood was all over my brand new blue T-shirt. David nearly passed out and fell out of the tree himself.

On that day Noel was the nearest thing to an adult at home. He was talking on the phone to his girlfriend, Lavonda. I just stood before him, dripping blood all over the floor, too stunned to speak! He took one look at my brand new blue, blood-soaked T-shirt and yelled, *"I gotta go! My brother's bleeding!"*

He made the wise decision to bypass Dr. Duncan's office and rush me directly to the Copper Queen Hospital. However, you can't rush anywhere in a '36 Chevy.

The nurses cut off my brand new blue T-shirt and washed me up good. I got a tetanus shot (it didn't hurt) and a huge bandage over my gash. They sent me to Dr. Duncan's office, shirtless. With a mirror clamped to his forehead, he sewed me up with just eighteen stitches.

I had a prize gash! Everybody wanted to see it—kids and grownups alike. I proudly showed it off. It's shaped like an "X."

For the first week, I had a hard time moving my arm, which meant I was excused from piano lessons. I milked that for all it was worth. I didn't practice the piano for six weeks!

One afternoon Mom spied me playing baseball down at Clawson School. I was busted. She blew her whistle. I meekly answered, "Coming."

"If you're healed enough to play baseball, you're healed enough to practice your piano."

Coincidentally, Mom was in the doctor's office—right at his desk—when the hospital called and told him I was on the way. Mom was there with a stiff-neck problem she'd complained about for months. Her head wouldn't turn without pain.

"That was the hospital," he told her. "Paul's had a little accident."

That simple comment shocked Mom so much that from that moment forward, her neck spun like a pinwheel on a windy day.

By the way, I worried I'd get in trouble for dripping blood all over the floor, but I didn't. And I didn't get in trouble for ruining my brand new blue T-shirt, either. In fact, that evening Dad went to the Dairy Queen and brought home a whole half gallon of soft ice cream. I got most of it.

• • •

Fifty Years Later Department: This entry is dedicated to my grandchildren Jake and Darby, who at ages 5 and 2, saw my scar and kissed it to make it all better.

• • •

*"If I had known my grandkids would be so much fun,
I would have had them first!"*

—Anonymous Grandparent

Toys for Boys (Tools) in Our Back Yard

Let's see. I narrowly missed sawing off a finger once. I smashed my thumb with a hammer more than once. I conked my knuckles under the hood of the pickup. "Oooh! That hurts every time I do it." I pinched the fat part of my finger with a pair of side cutters and raised painful, week-long welts. You'd think I'd learn. I still do it. I raised blisters by the score while wielding picks and shovels. Nasty splinters are my first cousins.

None of my friends on Seventh Street can boast like that!

We had tools, yes we did. Better yet, Dad taught us to use them. And he let us use them to our heart's content. Toys for boys.

Most of our tools were hand tools, long before electric/battery tools came along. Dad did have an electric table saw, but it was off limits. He had an electric grinder, and we were allowed to grind our fingers raw if we wanted.

Our wobbly workbench was outdoors, leaning against the front of the shed. A seventy-five pound bench vise was bolted to it. Next to it sat our anvil—the envy of any hard-working village blacksmith. With the workbench, vise and anvil we constructed whole cities, tore them down and started all over again.

When we put a pipe in the vise to saw it, we had to push our foot against the bench to keep it from pound-pound-pounding against the shed with every stroke.

Dad kept every tool he ever owned. If they broke, he fixed them—or made us fix them. If they wore out, he fashioned a new tool out of them. For instance, when a screwdriver became useless he ground it down to a point. Ta-da! Another scratch awl.

He rarely asked us what we were going to do with a certain tool. He let us find out if it worked or not. Here and there he offered a suggestion, which usually worked.

I don't think he ever bought a complete set of sockets. When he needed a certain size but didn't find it in one coffee can or another, he went down to the Sears and Roebuck and bought the one he needed. After several years, his set was almost complete.

He loved to tinker. Dad was a victim of the Great Depression, which helps explain why nothing got thrown out. Before he went to work for Immigration he was a machinist for the Southern Pacific Railroad.

My dad could fix anything from a stuck latch to a steam locomotive. Why didn't he ever shore up the workbench?

"...and he has filled him with the Spirit of God, with skill, ability and knowledge in all kinds of crafts..."

—Exodus 35:31

Chickens and Other Fowl Things
in Our Back Yard

Twice we had a chicken pen. "Free-range chickens." There were eggs to fetch every morning, but Dad usually did that because he liked to get up early.

Every so often, a neighbor sent a boy (or girl) to our house to ask to borrow an egg. *An* egg? No, Mom always gave them three or four. When it was time for payback Mom graciously said, "Oh, no, honey, you keep those. We have plenty. Now, you just take those on back to your mother."

By the way, do not throw eggs! That's worse than mixing chicken feed and dog food. Don't ask me how I know.

We pretty much ignored the chickens except for feeding, watering and catching them for dinner.

The second bunch of chickens we had were all started in a four-tier incubator. Home-grown eggs were carefully placed in the top layer under a warm lamp(s). When they hatched, the baby chicks were immediately transferred down to the next layer. We had to force them to drink.

Some days later, the chicks outgrew the second level and were transferred down to the third level where they learned to eat little granules of food. Finally, they got big enough for the bottom layer, where regular chicken feed was their diet.

The outdoor chicken pen was their last stop where hens started giving us more eggs. When the little roosters got big enough to irritate the neighbors first thing in the morning, we transferred them to our dinner table.

Noel also kept pigeons in a separate pen. Squab (baby pigeons) make for tasty lunches, but they're a lot of work. You have to prepare quite a few for just one meal. He also kept a pet crow out in the back yard. He and Neal clipped its wings to keep it from flying away. I'd say that crow hung around for at least a year. Noel had the silly notion that he'd teach it to talk.

I kept squab one year, but I wasn't too faithful about taking care of them so Dad opened up their door one day and let them fly away. For a couple of days they returned for dinner, but then...

We had some bunny rabbits, too. I really enjoyed those cute little bunnies—they tasted just like chicken.

The chicken pen also housed a few turkeys. I don't know why we didn't have more of them. Maybe it took more to feed them than it did to feed chickens, or maybe they didn't get along with the chickens.

And for a very brief time we had a peacock. Maybe a week. Only once did it spread its beautiful blue feathers. Oh, wow! Was that gorgeous! I don't know how that peacock got into Our Back Yard, nor how it left, but I'm sure we didn't eat him. I think my parents were "babysitting."

Fresh eggs, chickens, turkeys, quail, doves and rabbits. We ate them all. We shared with some of our Mexican friends across the line, too.

"When you reap the harvest of your land, do not reap to the very edges of your field or gather the gleanings of your harvest. Leave them for the poor and the alien..."

—Leviticus 23:22

How To Pluck A Chicken in Our Back Yard

Dad found a chunk of railroad tie, about three feet long. He drove two big nails into it, about half way, so that a chicken's neck would fit between them. That's where our chickens met their maker—a couple of hours before dinner. He fashioned a good-sized steel funnel to fit down a drain pipe, which he'd also rigged up.

To pluck a chicken, follow these fourteen easy steps.

1. Pick out a chicken and go catch it. That's always fun.

2. Stick its neck between the nails.

3. Stretch by its feet with your left hand.

4. Whack its head off with a small axe. That's fun, too.

5. Quickly, stick its neck down the drain.

6. Leave it alone till its feet quit motoring.

    (When its feet are still, then it's safe to pull it out without getting your hands all scratched up.)

7. Dip the chicken into a five gallon bucket of scalding water for about a minute.

8. With a brush of the hand, slide out as many feathers as you can while the flesh is still hot. There won't be much plucking left to do.

9. Pick out the remaining little pin feathers.

10. Cut the lower legs off with that axe.

11. Take the chicken into Mom. She'll clean it and fix you up a tasty fried chicken dinner. Yum-yum!

12. Don't let the dog get to the head or feet; throw them in the garbage along with your pile of feathers.

13. Turn the railroad tie on its side, so no one will fall on those big nails.

14. Leave the axe there for the next person.

We weren't supposed to cut the head off a chicken and let it run around like a chicken with its head cut off. But sometimes we did, particularly if a friend was in Our Back Yard watching. A few times it cost us a good scolding—and a cleanup chore if the chicken banged into the side of the house. It was worth it, though. Headless chickens are endless fascination.

Once in awhile Dad took some eggs and a plucked chicken or two across the line to Pastor Ibarra. While he was at it, he'd slip Pastor Ibarra a fifty-cent piece or maybe a silver dollar.

"Each day one ox, six choice sheep and some poultry were prepared for me..."

—Nehemiah 5:18

The Sweet and Sticky Garage
in Our Back Yard

Our garage was as busy as the house. It sat back about 20 feet or so from the house at the end of the Neatest Driveway on Earth. Inside it was divided in half. One half had a dirt floor where we parked the car. The other half was a low wooden platform, about eight inches above ground.

Mom and Dad kept Mason jars full of fruits and vegetables on the shelves that lined half the back wall. Cases of honey and beekeeping supplies were there as well.

Dad rigged up hot and cold running water for washing the clothes in our fancy Maytag wringer washer. He also rigged up a gas line and a little stove for heating up extracted honey.

Washing Clothes

Washing clothes was a family affair. Everyone pitched in one way or another. It usually took all of a morning to wash, rinse and hang clothes for a family of six (then five, then four). Later in the day, someone had to bring everything in from the clothes line. I did that by unpinning everything and stuffing them into a folded sheet. Then when everything was off the line, I took the sheet off, slung it over my shoulder and hauled it all inside.

Dad used such hot wash water that we needed a sawed-off broom handle to fish everything out of the machine. Everything went through the wringer three times into square tubs with less and less soapy water.

Fingers and hands went through a time or two, too.

"Ee-yow!"

It really didn't hurt that much. We just yowled for the heck of it, I guess. If you jammed your hand into the wringer on purpose, you were excused till "...it gets to feeling a little better." (wink)

Extracting Honey

Especially when there are as many hives as my dad had, extracting honey is much like harvesting farm crops. The whole family works together. It's serious business that must be done quickly. Dad's vacation time was dedicated to extracting honey and we did it in our garage.

Dad made a portable screen door, the size of the garage door, to give us a little (very little) breeze without all the bees coming in. It was nailed in place for the few days we needed it.

To get set up, the washing machine and all the tubs got shoved up against the wall. The car was left in the street and the extractor was set in its place.

The holding tank was washed, washed, washed and washed—with scalding hot water, no soap. Several layers of cheesecloth were stretched over the top and held down with clothespins spaced about a half inch apart.

The uncapping tub was set up to hold the capping, which is a wax covering that bees put over every cell. Dad removed the capping with a big, steam-heated uncapping knife and the honey flowed out. The capping dropped into a basket and we were free to chomp as much as we could hold.

Extra buckets were brought in. Empty supers were brought in. The little gas stove was fired up. The first super of honey frames was opened up, and away we went. Dad uncapping, kids extracting with a hand crank.

We placed the frames into a wire basket inside the extractor and took turns cranking. When we cranked, the inner basket spun and the honey whipped out. After a minute or so, we reversed the frames and cranked another minute. Honey from both sides of the frame was extracted.

Pretty soon that honey was poured into a five-gallon bucket, heated on the little stove and poured through the cheesecloth to strain out the poor dead bees and other debris. The heating/pouring/straining process was repeated the next day (with clean cheesecloth into a clean holding tank) and then the honey was ready for bottling.

Dad never said "no." If neighborhood kids wanted to come in and watch, they were welcome—encouraged and invited, actually.

"Wanna chew some beeswax with honey all over it? No problem. Help yourself."

"Wanna stick your finger under the pour spout? Here you go. Right here. Tastes good, eh?"

If Dad decided someone was in the way or getting a little unruly, he whacked off a chunk of honeycomb and wrapped it in a couple of sheets of wax paper.

"Do you think your parents would like some honeycomb?"

"Yeah! Sure!"

"Well, here, take this to them. Be careful now. Don't drop it."

"Thanks, Mr. Nichols!"

He never said they couldn't stay.

The way to thrill Dad was to volunteer to help extract honey. Or just ask permission to come over and watch, maybe learn something about bees. His diaries note several names of boys and men who learned to keep bees under Dad's careful, watchful, encouraging eye. He entertained plenty of visitors and out-of-town relatives out there in his "honey house." Of course, we kids at home never volunteered; I'm talking about curious friends and neighbors.

Quite often beginning beekeepers brought their hive or two over and Dad let them extract their own honey. He had the equipment—and the boys—to crank the extractor.

Now here's a neat deal. When it was cleanup time, we set the sticky buckets and tools outside and let the bees lick them clean. They did a great job of it, too.

One last thing: Dad melted all the extra beeswax, poured it into a square mold, and at the end of the year shipped it to a bee supply company in exchange for more wax foundations for next year's hives.

We extracted honey two times a year; once in awhile more. It was not easy work. I forgot to tell you yet that we made many trips back and forth between home and Slaughter's Ranch to shuttle beehives. That was the easy part.

•   •   •

Sweet Perfection Department: Honey is the only perfect food. It is the only food that will never spoil. It has been found in some of the ancient Egyptian pyramids just as delicious as the day it was placed there.

•   •   •

"Eat honey, my son, for it is good; honey from the comb is sweet to your taste."

—Proverbs 24:13

We Fired Up Burn Barrels in Our Back Yard

Many 50s back yards had a burn barrel. People burned just about anything they wanted, including oily rags, gasoline, old tires, paint thinner and lead-based paint. Most people only burned their yard debris and some occasional paper like gift wrap. Most people—*but in Our Back Yard*...

For Our Back Yard, Dad brought home 55-gallon barrels that once held thick, sticky, oily packing tar. What better place to clean it than in Our Back Yard? I always volunteered to help, because we're talking fire here. Dad turned the barrel upside down and let me get a roaring fire going to burn out all that tar. How can you be a Nichols boy and not bang a hot barrel just to watch clouds of sparks go sailing up? How can you be a Nichols boy and not stoke three times more wood than necessary just to hear the fire echo out of the barrel? That's attention-getting! Neighborhood kids slowly rode their bikes past our yard. Sometimes they hung on the alley fence to watch and lust.

It was a masterful way to clean out a barrel, though. That we were polluting half the town didn't matter. The word "pollution" didn't exist when I lived at 1122 Seventh Street.

Speaking of pollution: the Phelps-Dodge smelter in Douglas was a world class producer of pollution. Its twin stacks poured out heavy, stinky, sulphur-laden smoke twenty-four hours a day.

On a day without wind, the heavy smoke settled close to the ground, often resting all over Douglas. It irritated your eyes, nose and throat. It was foul tasting and harsh smelling. Whatever we were doing outside—kids and grown ups alike—we just kept on doing, not the least bit worried that all kinds of violent diseases were secretly cultivating inside us.

It was during one of those times that I first heard the expression, "It smells like money." Yeah, money for Phelps-Dodge. But Douglas wouldn't be there if the smelter wasn't there. Phelps-Dodge was the main employer, so we all put up with that acrid smoke. Usually it blew north, anyway. Let the people in Elfrida deal with it.

In Our Back Yard we prepared one special barrel every year for my other sister who lived in Africa...

Eunice's Barrel Began in Our Back Yard

"There's the postman," Mom said. "Go out and get the mail please?"

Ruth or I enthusiastically yelled back through our screen door, *"We got a letter from Eunice!"*

She wasn't really our sister, but that's how I always thought of her. I'd say Eunice is about twenty years older than I. She was a member of our church and a protestant missionary to French West Africa, which is now Nigeria.

Eunice went overseas for four years at a time, then spent a year back in the US looking for financial and prayer support for her ministry in Africa. Ruth and I always looked forward to her coming home. We had to get all cleaned up, put on some Sunday School clothes and go down to the train depot to pick her up.

When she was home, 1122 Seventh Street was hers. It didn't matter that we had only two bedrooms and just one bathroom, my parents provided everything she needed: a couch to sleep on, all the quiet time she wanted, a dining room table for writing and studying, a slide projector to organize her slides and all the home-cooked Mexican food she could hold.

Mr. Louis Mason, who owned the Southern Arizona Auto Company, loaned her a used car for the year, too. Mr. Mason was also a member of our church. He didn't attend services regularly, but he was active on committees, in meetings and adult Sunday School. Most of all he was a kind and generous man. He was always nice to Mom. The Southern Arizona Auto Company donated lots of "stuff" to the church and to Eunice. One time, Mr. Mason attended a church business meeting and donated a used Pontiac station wagon to the church, but for the exclusive use of the Pastor (Morgan) and his family. It was light green.

Eunice and Mom at the train depot, early 50s.

I really liked Eunice, but have long since lost contact with her. She was single all her life. That was lucky for me, because we "dated" a couple of times. That is, I'd save up some allowance (and beg Mom to lend me just three more dollars) and we'd go out for lunch together. And Eunice always paid for lunch.

She encouraged me to consider a missionary career. I never committed but I promised to pray for her a lot. And I did pray for her—but not a lot.

One of my distinct visions of Eunice is seeing her on her knees, praying into our couch—for a long time.

It was exciting to find her letters in the mail box. They came on thin, blue paper. There were folding instructions printed on it. When you folded the sheet just so, it became the envelope, too. So first you wrote the letter on one side only, then folded it for mailing. Short dark blue stripes ran along the front folded edges and bold lettering proclaimed "Correo Aereo" and "Air Mail."

Eunice's mother lived in Elfrida, north of Douglas, but Eunice only stayed out there briefly. She traveled around Arizona during her furlough, visiting Baptist churches in every town along Highway 80, and plenty more, too. She always came back to our house. Well, why not? She was my other sister. She is the heart and foundation of my interest in missions.

Eunice's barrel got special treatment after we burned it clean. Lucky me, I got to crawl inside with some lead-based aluminum paint and a four-inch brush and paint it. Then I painted the outside and the lid. When I finishesd it was gleaming silver in the Arizona sunlight. I was, too. I looked like a Tom Sawyer character.

You know how I cleaned up? I poured gasoline all over my hands and arms and dissolved it all away. I wiped myself down with a towel soaked in gasoline. Then I washed up with a couple of watery globs of Tide. I walked around—outside—smelling like gasoline for two hours, but I had to take a bath and clean out the tub if I wanted to sit down at the dinner table.

During the year, church folks gathered supplies. You name it, it went into Eunice's shiny barrel. The premier items were some cans of Dad's honey, lots of flour tortillas, and a year's supply of Picante sauce. New clothes/used clothes, blankets, coffee, American sugar, new books, cookies, chewing gum and candy, pasta packages, Lipton tea bags, ink for her pen, a box of those blue letters/envelopes,—wow, there were a lot of things for her barrel. Nothing that spoiled was allowed to go.

Certain things had to be wrapped certain ways to prevent spillage or breakage and Dad lovingly got them that way.

When it was fully and tightly packed, Dad put the top on and carefully painted her African address on it. Two or three men from the church came over and helped heft it into his pickup. He took it to the freight depot and Eunice received it about a month later. It wasn't long before we received a glowing letter of gratitude.

Her name is Eunice Peevey.

"This service that you perform is not only supplying the needs of God's people but is also overflowing in many expressions of thanks to God."

—2 Corinthians 9:12

Dangerous Supers Barrel in Our Back Yard

And we cleaned beehive supers in the burn barrels. *Viciously* cleaned them. Supers are the individual sections of a beehive. In the course of a year, a number of bad things can happen inside them, including disease, termites, foul brood and worms.

So Dad mounted a cleaned-out 55-gallon barrel on a stack of bricks and filled it with water. *Oh, boy!* We tossed a handful of milk carton bottoms underneath, jammed a bunch of scrap lumber on top of that and set the stuff ablaze. That was the fun part and the only part when Dad let us participate. When the water got to boiling, he shooed everyone away and emptied a box of lye into it.

He dipped each super into the boiling lye water for a couple of minutes to decontaminate it. Cleansing them was usually a half day project, and there were plenty of half days! Not only did the lye kill all the germs, but it loosened a sizeable amount of (lead-based) paint, too. Dad let me stick more lumber into the fire to keep the water boiling, but otherwise I had to stay away, because the bubbling lye water might splash onto me and… well, I've seen the holes it chewed in Dad's shirt sleeves. When the supers cooled down, I was responsible to scrape off loose paint.

Of all the activities that went on in our back yard, boiling the supers was the only one when other people were not allowed. No kids, no adults, no nobody. There were plenty of angels, though, because it was dangerous work, and no one was ever hurt. Considering the wobbly, homemade, make-shift contraptions Dad rigged up to get the job done, there *had* to be angels around

A few days after they dried we set up a different contraption (a table-like thing) and repainted them. Then they were ready for another year out at Slaughter's Ranch.

I painted this beehive. Dad did the artwork inside the lid, which I'm holding. Looks like I'm about 8 or 9 years old then. The picture was taken in the Mason's yard next door at 1124.

"Cleanse me with hyssop, and I will be clean;
wash me, and I will be whiter than snow."

—Psalm 51:7

Dad's Garden(s) in Our Back Yard

"Well, I guess I won't do that again," Dad said one morning.

"What?" Noel wondered out loud.

"Plant corn in the front row."

The corn was so abundant that year, that we had a hard time getting to the rest of the garden. And we had to cut out a couple of stalks because they were in the way of the garbage cans.

Four rows out by the alley. You can plant a lot of food in just four rows. Dad used Mrs. Mason's fence to guide his pretty sweet pea flowers, then planted four rows of vegetables.

He usually had a row of corn and half a row of green beans. Tomatoes dominated the rest of the garden, but there was some yellow squash and zucchini, too. There were a lot of tomatoes. Dad loved tomatoes. He planted cucumbers one year. And failed at watermelon one time. He planted a bacon bush one year, but no luck. They say you can't grow those in the desert.

He didn't plant every year. If we had had a rototiller, he might have. But he had to turn every inch by shovel, which was hard, time-consuming work. Because we bought cheap vegetables over across the line, he only gardened about every two years. However, he always planted his sweet peas and at least two pet tomato plants.

Smart dad I had. In the years there was no garden, he let me dig holes there. That turned his dirt pretty good.

Butch Barrett and I almost made it through to China on the other side of the earth one summer, but just before we got there, Dad said it was time to fill in the hole.

"You can start another one a little closer to the back fence, if you want," he told us. So we did.

"Just don't dig so deep this time, dig wider." So that's what we did. We didn't find any buried treasure, so before long we filled it in and went off to other adventures.

Gee, what a nice dad I had. He let us dig another one about midway between those last two. That was the year before we reaped that bountiful crop of corn.

Dad never let on when he pulled one over on us, he just let us plow his garden for him.

Please Note: "the other side of the earth" is about four feet away.

"For as the soil makes the sprout come up and a garden causes seeds to grow, so the Sovereign Lord will make righteousness and praise spring up before all nations."

—Isaiah 61:11

The Shed in Our Back Yard

"Where's that thing?"

"It's out in the shed."

Depending on what the "thing" was, we knew right where to look. Out by the alley, a three-room shed row kept tools, extra things and a bedroom. The shed was about 30 feet long, unpainted. If your thing was a tool, it was in the tool room. If it was an old blanket or an old book, it was in the middle room. The other room was Neal's bedroom first, then Noel's bedroom, then mine. No girls allowed.

The tool shed was Dad's outdoor "office." Tools weren't organized, because if they were we couldn't find them. It was easier to plow through boxes and coffee cans till we found what we wanted. The electric, belt-driven table saw was in the tool shed on a home-made stand.

Dad prepared new frames for his beehives in there, a favorite task for cool or rainy weather. When we were small enough, the tool shed was a good hiding place.

Another good hiding place was a huge crate in that middle room. It was so big it had two lids, side by side. I have no idea what its original purpose was, but Mom stored sheets and blankets, clothing, knitting and tons of McCall's and Butterick patterns. The room always smelled like mothballs, which were liberally dumped into that crate.

We had a virtual library in there, too. Hardy Boys mysteries, classic literature and poetry, Bible study materials. We never threw away the *National Geographic*. They ended up in the shed. Years worth! *Look, Life, The Saturday Evening Post, Reader's Digest* and *Boys Life* were out there, too. If doctors, dentists and barbers were to see those magazines, they'd cringe with jealousy.

Where Dad found the desk for our bedroom, I don't know, but it was solid enough to last past Neal, Noel and me. There was a dresser and a military bed for us. A lone pull-string light bulb lit up the room. A little electric heater warmed us in winter. Concrete floor. No carpet, no rugs, no insulation.

I was eleven or twelve years old when I went into Noel's room one day for who knows what reason. I guess I was just poking around my big brother's room looking for something interesting. I didn't find anything. Well, except for a pack of Lucky Strike cigarettes. Hmmm. I decided to try a puff. I tore open the package and dug out a cigarette. I took my first deep drag…and for the next six hours everything I saw looked like green pea pudding.

Later that day, Noel tattled. Mom scolded me harshly. "Hey, I had an open pack right on the desk," Noel said. "If you had gotten one of those, I would have never known."

I didn't like to go in there when it was Noel's stinky room. He kept a Folgers coffee can in there because he was too lazy to walk into the house to tinkle. How he put up with that smell is beyond me.

When it was my room, I was smarter than Noel: at night I just stepped out the door.

I made a major improvement to our bedroom when I moved in. I added a little white plastic radio. I only listened at night, because after dark, certain AM radio stations reduced their wattage and others increased. I listened to American rock 'n' roll music from XELO in Juarez, Chihuahua, Mexico or KOMA in Oklahoma City. Sometimes KTKT in Tucson played for me. "Color Radio!" It was available in the daytime, too, but the dial had to be perfectly on the dot.

KOMA boasted, "24 hours of music! 24 hours of news! The only station in America on the air 48 hours a day!" XELO played a Spanish coffee commercial too many hours a night. "Café Combate…" That jingle still drives me crazy. I listened to plenty of Mexican music on that station, too. Love it.

We needed a basketball backboard, so Dad built one. I think Neal helped. It was the ugliest backboard in the history of the sport. Dad put it on the roof above the tool shed door. He used various widths of lumber and spaced the boards a couple of inches apart until it was about 6 feet tall. The thing looked like a fence standing on end. He made it that way so the wind wouldn't blow it off the roof. I sure had a lot of explaining to do to snickering friends who came by and saw it. None of us were good basketball players, anyway.

Dad always looked for a way to make things work better, but his backboard was a good example of "If it ain't broke, fix it till it is."

Our three-room shed was our warm and wonderful place. I hammered and sawed and went to Treasure Island and learned to love Norman Rockwell and sank roots into Mexican music and rested and earned an A in English homework and started my first novel and...

"Be at rest once more, O my soul, for the Lord has been good to you."

—Psalm 116:7

The Sound of Sunrise

Summer mornings in Cochise County began about five or five-thirty, when it was cool(ish). The temperature was down around 75 degrees. The sun broke over D Hill, promising another hot, sunny day. If I slept all night with my window open, sometimes I was awakened by music drifting across the border from Mexico. We heard some sort of a drum and bugle corps, marching back and forth on the Agua Prieta community baseball field, practicing for something.

Ta-dup. Ta-dup. Ta-duppety-duppety dup. Snare drums played the same rhythm over and over again while the bugles, off-key by the way, played march music. I never saw them but, as their intriguing Mexican marches wafted across the border, I imagined dusty brown boots tromping across the solid dirt outfield. I pictured about a dozen marchers or so, most of them drummers. I knew when they were facing Seventh Street and when they were headed the other way. I pulled a sheet up over my sleepy head and just listened.

Did you ever get a song stuck in your head for several irritating hours? Sometimes the rhythm of those drums got stuck in my head and I marched around to the beat of them for half a day.

Ta-dup. Ta-dup. Ta-duppety-duppety dup.

During medieval times, people took the name of their trade as their last name. Turner, Carpenter, Taylor, Smith. So let's call Dad "Mr. Tinker."

I woke up on summer mornings to hear him outside tinkering away on something. Maybe his head was stuck under the hood of his pickup. Maybe he was filling a wooden peach crate with garden vegetables. Maybe he was painting beehives or getting frames ready for a new crop of honey. Sometimes I think washing a small load of clothes was another one of his hobbies.

Regardless of his task, he was whistling "Turkey in the Straw." It was the only tune I ever heard him whistle, and I heard him whistling it many a morning. I got up and went outside with him. If I didn't have a hole to dig or a board to saw, Dad found me an easy morning chore. I tinkered on something, just like my dad. Pretty soon we went in for a bowl of oatmeal.

Summer or winter, 1122 Seventh Street had a beautiful sound that I'm willing to bet no other home on earth ever heard. It was a tender sound; special, almost reverent. And simple.

Every morning of my life at 1122 Seventh Street, if he wasn't working the graveyard shift, Dad poured Mom a cup of black coffee and carried it to her bedside.

"Morning," he said quietly.

Mom opened her eyes and said, "Hi, honey."

"There you go," he said, setting the coffee on her night stand.

Kiss.

"Satisfy us in the morning with your unfailing love, that we may sing for joy and be glad all our days."

—Psalm 90:14

Two Sweet Women

There are two sweet women I really want you to meet. Of course, I have no idea where they are now, but I can pretty well promise I'll introduce you when we all get to heaven.

Betina and Blanca are sisters who were once-a-week housekeepers in our home. They attended *La Iglesia Asambleas de Dios* in Agua Prieta where they lived. Sometimes they were around for our big dinners, too. Not to join us, but to clean up afterward. Well, they ate all they wanted, but in the kitchen.

My parents loved them to pieces, and rightly so. They were faithful and careful girls who were the next best things to cousins. I'll bet Mom and Dad wished they got as much housecleaning out of us kids. They had the run of the house and occasionally were sort of like babysitters to me and Ruth.

They ironed and did windows, too.

Betina and Blanca walked about four dusty miles to our house. They worked non-stop all day, cleaning up after people like me. We sat down together for lunch like family. They spoke broken English and we spoke worse Spanish, but we got along well. In the evenings, Dad gave them a few dollars and drove them back home. I think he paid them a little more than what most of the Douglas housekeepers received. Still, it was pauper's wages.

Betina, the older, took care of our home for a few years until she went to college in Tijuana. Can you believe that in Tijuana, the sin city of Baja California, there is (or was) an Assembly of God Bible college? That's where she went. Then Blanca took over just as efficiently.

Both Betina and Blanca got Christmas gifts from my parents for several years. Dad was a guest "preacher" in their church several times. Blanca hugged me when I graduated from high school.

One of my friends at A.J. Bayless grocery store gave me a great recipe for hot sauce. I got all the ingredients together and made myself a Mason jar full of the stuff. I kept adding a certain pepper and daintily tasted till I broke out in a sweat. "Aah! Perfect."

"*¿Quieres a probar mi salsa, Blanca?*" I offered proudly. ("Do you want to taste my sauce, Blanca?")

She tasted a big ol' spoonful, smacked her lips a little, thought about it.

"*S'okay, pero…*" She ground up half a handful of those peppers and stirred them in really good. She gulped another spoonful. "*Mmmm. Mejor,*" she approved.

It was my turn to taste. I cautiously sipped a tiny bit.

When the wax in my ears quit melting and my voice box started working again, I got up off the floor and wheezed, "That stuff is great!"

I always loved Blanca.

"Taste and see that the Lord is good…"

—Psalm 34:8

God Bless America

The 4tha July is the best holiday of them all. Plenty of sunshine. A hundred five degrees. Long days, short nights. Picnics, parades, pretty girls at the pool. Most likely a baseball game at Clawson School.

On summer holidays, the 15th Street Park was always crowded with picnicking families. On the 4tha July, after hanging out at the swimming pool next to the park, we casually cut through the park about four o'clock, hoping somebody would recognize us and wave. "You boys want a hot dog?" Polite boys only took three.

Our family didn't have 4tha July picnics because Dad worked the day shift or we extracted honey.

But that evening, Dad jammed eight or ten boys and girls into the back of his pickup and took us to the football stadium for fireworks. In Douglas, the sun sets so late that fireworks don't start until about ten o'clock. In the meantime, a big community, red-white-and-blue affair started the city freedom celebration.

Children's groups took turns on wobbly risers to sing patriotic American songs into a pathetic little PA system. The lower-grade Catholic students from Loretto School always—*always*—danced a May Pole, and I liked that.

Each student carried a long, colored crepe paper streamer around and around the tall pole. Their nuns, with hands clasped on their tummies, proudly coached them through the maze of ribbons. Before long they presented a nifty red, white and blue pole. How'd they do that? I liked the year they braided three poles at once.

The American Legion Drum and Bugle Corps blared up and down the field and veterans marched Old Glory around for everybody to see and salute. The mayor added his two cents worth. His speech, usually inaudible through that squawky PA contraption, meant fireworks were not far behind. By nine-thirty, everybody in town was within four blocks of the stadium.

And somebody had waited long enough. Firecrackers went off behind the bleachers. Fidgety kids tore off in the direction of all the popping. Some more went off in the parking lot. Somebody in 15th Street Park fired off M-80s. Across the street a few whistling bottle rockets took off and more kids took off for that.

"You kids stay here where I can see you! Hey! Come back over here, young man!"

"Aw, Mom. Everybody else is..."

"You're not everybody else. You stay right here. I don't want you blowing your hand off. Or putting your eye out."

"What time is it, anyway?" Even the adults were restless for fireworks. "They'll be starting any ti..."

Boom!

Finally. What we were there for. We plopped cross-legged onto the football field and oohed and aahed for half an hour under an umbrella of bright, loud, colorful explosions.

God bless America the Beautiful.

"I will walk about in freedom, for I have sought out your precepts."

—Psalm 119:45

Only Three Dozen Chocolate Chip Cookies

I knew, I knew, I knew I was already in big trouble.

I was doing the dishes after school one day. Mom had made the mistake of baking six dozen chocolate chip cookies for some church get-together. Worse yet, she left them right out there on the kitchen table. They were hardly four feet away from where I was working. Mom wasn't home for some reason, and that meant Rule #1: *"No cookies without my permission!"*

The sight of them! The smell of them! I was in downtown Temptation City.

I only took one. Yum, yum! I only took another one. They were far and away the best chocolate chip cookies I'd ever eaten. Soft and chewy with lots of chips! They had walnuts in them, too!

They were big! I *love* big chocolate chip cookies! They were delicious! I only had another one.

By the time my brother Noel got home from school, I only had a few more.

"Wow!" he said, What are these cookies for? "

"I dunno," I said.

"Can we eat one?"

"Yeah, sure," I told him. He took a couple and headed out the back door.

Well, he took a couple, so I only took a couple, too.

Wouldn't you know it? Mom came home about then. Her eyes went straight to that plate of cookies. Her mouth dropped open, her eyes bulged out. "What happened to all those cookies?" she demanded.

"Uh, well, Noel ate some," I confessed. Out the door she bolted, steaming after Noel. My mind was zipping around trying to figure out a way to vaporize myself. Then I heard Noel yell, "Paul said we could have some. I only had two."

Back in the door Mom bolted. "How many of those did you eat"? she demanded again.

"Mom, I couldn't help it," I pleaded. "They were just *so good!*" Her shoulders dropped just a little, a crook of a smile almost appeared, an eyebrow flicked, oh, so faintly. No spanking for me. But she got right back to her anger.

"Those cookies were for..." she thundered. On and on she went about why she made them, how many she made *("...six dozen! And now there's not even half that!")*, when she needed them, who was to have them, what it would take to make some more.

Hell hath no fury like a Mom who's lost three dozen chocolate chip cookies.

I knew, I knew, I knew I was already in big trouble. Sure enough— I was. BIG trouble!

"Not another cookie!" But only for the rest of my life.

She sentenced me to enough chores to keep me busy till I graduated from college.

"And you're grounded!" But only till the Lord comes back.

"Chocolate is not just a food—it's a state of mind!"

—First Commandment, Chocolaholics Anonymous

Big Brothers! What Good Are They?

When it was time for a slingshot battle, up on the garage roof we went. From there we loaded our pockets with chinaberries. They were marble size and hard. Dark green and hard. Pockets loaded, we climbed down and took up stations behind a fence or a tree or a stack of supers and fired away at each other.

"Hah! Missed!"

"Ow! Who shot that?"

The secret to a great slingshot battle is to wait for someone to innocently come out the back door. *Pop! Pop!* Then it doesn't matter whose side you're on.

"Hey! Don't! Mom, they're shooting chinaberries at me!"

"You boys stop th… Now *stop it*, I said. You're liable to put somebody's eye out!"

"You're mean!" Ruth said.

I hit mom right in the seat one time. Armando and Richie Verdugo were watching and grinning. It was a beautiful shot from my tree house.

"Uh-oh," I worried.

She never flinched. She kept her head high and marched on into the house.

From the garage roof, I got Dad in the upper arm once. He looked up and kept on walking. Unfortunately, Noel and one of his friends were up in his tree house. They retaliated on Dad's behalf. "Hey! No fair!" I retreated to the far end of the roof, but not before one of them created a welt on the back of my arm. Didn't those mean older boys know they might put my eye out?

One hot noontime, Neal, my other mean brother, and I climbed up on the shed roof. We arrived just as Mom leaned out the back door and called, "Neal and Paul. Your lunch is on the table." Neal jumped down into the alley, ready to eat.

"Now you jump," he told me.

I took a look. I figured it was about forty feet to the ground, maybe a lot more. That was a little further than I wanted to jump.

"I'll just climb down by the fence," I said.

"Nope. You gotta jump."

"No, really. I'll just climb down."

"Oh no you won't," he proclaimed.

For the next hot fifteen minutes, he stymied every effort I made to get down without jumping. I tried slipping down when he wasn't looking. But he was looking and chased me back up. I wandered the edges, looking for a way to get down. If he saw my little tears, maybe he thought they were sweat. He blocked every escape.

Every few minutes I looked down again. Maybe it wasn't so far after all. Nope, it was pretty far. In fact, my original estimate was wrong: it was about a hundred feet.

"Hurry up. Mom wants us to come in and eat."

"I can't. It's too far."

"It's not that far. Just jump."

"Come on, Neal," I whimpered. "Just let me climb down. *Pleeeeze.*"

"Sit on the edge and jump!"

"It's too hot to sit on." Arizona roofing material creates heat waves so thick and hot you can fold them up and use them in the oven.

I fearfully decided to either stay up there and cook myself till I starved to death, or jump and only break my legs. I squatted and nervously looked down at the alley. It sure was a long way down there. Finally I sat on the edge for a couple of hot seconds and pushed myself off, landing solidly on both feet just seven feet down.

No big deal. Neal and I swaggered in to eat.

"How good and pleasant it is when brothers live together in unity!...For there the Lord bestows his blessing."

—Psalm 133:1 and 3

Saturday Afternoon Matinees

The 40s and 50s spawned a wonderful American ritual that only lasted about twenty-five years. But in any town worth its salt, everyone between eight and eighteen went to the Saturday Afternoon Matinee. Nothing came before it. Not homework, not church, not scouts (Boy or Girl/Cub or Brownie), not music lessons, best friends, sports—not even chores. *Every kid in America* was at the Saturday Afternoon Matinee.

Douglas boasted two theaters: the Grand on the corner of G Avenue and Twelfth Street, and the Lyric between F and G Avenues on Tenth Street. For Saturday Afternoon Matinees, we went to the elegant Grand Theatre.

About 12:30 we lined up out in the heat and yelled "Hey! No cuts!" until we plunked down a dime for a ticket. We milled around the lobby deciding which big candy bar to choose. Or maybe a tall paper bag of popcorn. We also got a tall Pepsi without a top. "That's fifteen cents, please."

Thick, plush red carpet that withstood a ka-jillion pairs of dirty tennies covered the lobby and the staircases leading to the balcony. Globs of bubble gum dotted the floor and double-covered the bottom of every seat in the house. Heavy red curtains covered the screen till the first reel started.

A certain decorum and conduct was expected of us. Inside the Grand everyone chose a seat. There were no parents there, so we moved to another seat, then another, then ran up into the balcony, spilling popcorn and Pepsi every which way. We spotted some friends downstairs and ran back to sit with them. If they moved, too, that was okay. We took their seats or sat with whoever got there ahead of us. Moving around all afternoon was all part of the Matinee. There were no parents there.

First came a newsreel, almost always featuring a smiling, waving, golfing President Eisenhower. Some of our baseball heroes were shown swatting homers. Weary American GIs in some place called

Korea marched across the screen with Lucky Strikes dangling from their lips. The newsreel usually featured a slick, futuristic invention—a sleek gray car, a machine that washed all the dishes at once, an automatic ironer, a mathematical calculator about the size of a store—some clunky gizmo promising to make life easier someday.

Loud talking was the preferred noise at this time. But if you blew into the end of an empty Red Hots box, you pierced the darkness with a shrill, ear-splitting whistle. Somewhere, someone answered the same way. Others responded, too. Still others went to the candy counter to get a box of their own. They didn't eat their Red Hots, they just mixed them with the gum on the floor and joined the chorus. Somehow all that racket made the house lights flash three times. That was the signal to stop the noise—or else.

"Eh, What's up, Doc?" Next, two or three cartoons. Looney Tunes were everyone's favorite. Tom and Jerry were popular and so were Woody Woodpecker and Popeye.

Then a serial. Oh, those serials were fabulous. They're the reason kids went every week: to see how Captain America or Rocket Man got out of last week's cliffhanger. We had lots of heroes to choose from, too. Batman and Robin, Superman, Zorro, The Shadow and several others.

Another cartoon or two. Sometimes we were treated to a short Three Stooges movie or we howled at the Bowery Boys.

Cartoons we already saw were a chance to tease the girls. Dangling rubber spiders were a favorite for that. A blast from a Red Hots box directly behind a pretty girl's ear was good for a chase through the balcony. A Saturday matinee is no matinee at all if all you do is sit still and watch the screen.

At a Saturday matinee, never eat the whole bag of popcorn. Save about a third. Then wad up the bag around it and see how many times it will fly across the crowd before it breaks open.

Finally, the feature movie: a western starring Johnny Mack Brown, Tom Mix, Whip Wilson, Lash LaRue, Gene Autry, Rex Allen, the Lone Ranger and Tonto, Roy Rogers and Dale Evans. Or even the new guy, John Wayne.

I liked black and white westerns because they confirmed my belief that the entire country was a desert. Tree-lined streets, white picket fences and lush green fields were nothing but a myth. There was nothing like that in Cochise County and B-movie westerns didn't have them, either.

About 4:00 we all scattered out into the bright desert sunshine. Anyone who went home without gum stuck to his shoes was a lucky one indeed. When we got back to Seventh Street we strapped on our shiny pistols and set out looking for that sinister, land-grabbing banker. The one with the black hat.

"Eh, don't take life so seriously, Doc."

—Bugs Bunny

God's Will for Your Life for Just $6

I got lucky one summer. The Valenzuelas asked me to watch over their yard while they spent the summer on their ranch down in Mexico.

"Paul, we'll pay you ninety dollars for the summer. That's the same as a dollar a day. Is that okay?"

I hurried home and told Mom, who said, "Well, don't you think that's a little too much to pull a few weeds and pick up the mail?" I figured there was no such thing as "a little too much."

In the meantime, my "sister" Eunice was praying. She was home from Africa and in an emotional dither about whether to stay home and begin a radio ministry, or return to Africa.

For ninety dollars, I had to keep the weeds out of the yard and collect the mail and the Douglas Daily Dispatch. I'd say that was free money.

But there was a problem. Their yard was dirt, front and back. Soft and sandy. No grass. Except for a couple of large bushes in the front, there was no other growth. Weed heaven!

First day. I picked up the paper and the mail. No weeds.

Second day. Same thing.

Seventh day. Couple of little ragweeds that can wait.

Day fourteen. "I'd better get to all these weeds while they're still easy to pull."

Day twenty-one. Tall ragweeds everywhere. And more on the way!

Day twenty-two to ninety. I couldn't keep up. I chopped one, three sprang up. My hoe wasn't big enough, my shovel not sharp enough, my rake not wide enough.

"Oh, man," I cried, "I'm doing all this hard work and they're not gonna pay me!" Most of those rascally weeds had grown two feet high. I decided to concentrate on the front and sides.

"Hey, Paul. Whatcha doing? I thought you were going to play baseball with us."

I watched those weeds grow before my eyes!

"Hey, Paul. You want to go over to the store for something cold to drink?"

Just the slightest sprinkle of rain last night and the weeds grew half an inch—across!

"Come on, Paul, it's Saturday, man! Let's go to the show."

And Jack thought he had a beanstalk problem!

With just a week left, I had most of them down, but miniature weeds had sprouted! Oh, brother! They were too green and too close to the house to set them on fire. Weed spray was unheard of.

In my mind's eye, I pictured Eunice praying. In my wildest, sweaty fantasy I prayed she was praying for a miracle for me.

Chop. Whack. Pile them up. *Chop. Whack.* Pile them up. *Chop. Whack.* Pile them up.

Their yard was a mess. When the family came home I had all their mail neatly packed in a clean box, and the newspapers stacked in order. That didn't count. Their yard was a mess.

"Paul. We're disappointed. We're only going to give you sixty dollars. And we want you to get rid of those piles you left in the back yard."

Apparently Mom forgot I had earlier said ninety dollars, because she was impressed that I came home with three twenty dollar bills. I didn't tell her that I had not done a good job. I didn't tell her I was undisciplined and unreliable. I just showed her the money.

"Remember son, you need to set aside six dollars for tithe."

"I know."

"Why don't you give it to Eunice?"

So I gave Eunice six dollars tithing money. And Mom made me buy some new school clothes.

Eunice decided to stay in America and begin a radio ministry. "It was Paul's six dollars," she told my mother in front of me.

"Huh?"

"I asked the Lord to send me six dollars if He wanted me to stay here. *Specifically six dollars.* Otherwise, I would consider it His will for me to go back to Nigeria. And Paul gave me six dollars." She patted my shoulder. "And not too soon, either." Eunice moved to Oklahoma City and began a little weekly radio ministry that lasted into the '80s.

I disappointed the Valenzuelas. I disappointed myself. I disappointed the Lord, but it wasn't beneath Him to graciously take my little gift and answer Eunice's prayer.

"...not because of anything we have done, but because of his own purpose and grace..."

—2 Timothy 1:9

Do Not Try This At Home!

Doug Foster's east side fence was across Bonita Avenue from Early's Grocery store.

One summer morning when his parents weren't home, six or seven of us concocted the idea of shooting CO_2 cylinders all the way across the street, about thirty feet.

First, we brought a cylinder to Our Back Yard because 1122 had the only bench vise in the neighborhood. I hacksawed off its back end. We noisily gangled back to Doug's house and stuffed it full of match heads and a paper fuse. We slipped the cylinder into a three-foot pipe, propped that up, lit the fuse and "*Ka-whish!*" Off it went.

"Bling!" A good hit in the center of Early's brick wall. It rebounded and spun along the street. "Blink-edy, Blink-edy, Tink. Tink. Tink."

"Hey, neat! Let's do that again!" One of us chased it down and we did it again.

"*Ka-whish!*" Off it went. "Bling!" It hit the brick wall. "Blink-edy, Blink-edy, Tink. Tink. Tink." One of us chased it down and we did it again.

We even devised a simple and effective safety plan: "Get back, I'm getting ready to light it. *Behind it*, Dodo!"

It wasn't long before we realized that it was probably easy to hit the wall of Clawson School, too. But were match heads enough fuel? Hmmm. How about firecracker powder? Armando always had firecrackers.

"Hey, yeah! Let's try it and see."

With match heads it goes "*Ka-whish.*" With firecracker powder it goes "*Ka-Whoosh!*" And it goes further. Faster. But unfortunately, it only goes about half way into the school yard, coming up short of the building by several feet. How were we going to reach the building? More powerful firecrackers, of course—like the M-80s in Doug's house.

We got the powder out of three or four and...they worked great! We put two cylinders on the roof and one went clear over the school.

Who's bright idea was it to empty the powder out of .22 bullet shells? Who cares? We twisted the slugs out and poured the gunpowder into the cylinder. I'd say about eight bullets went into that cylinder, maybe more.

"Ka-Boom!" The whole pipe went flailing into the street. The cylinder was nowhere to be found even though we looked and looked. Wow! Where had it gone? Eventually, I picked up the pipe and found the cylinder split down the middle and wedged inside the pipe, which now looked like a snake after its lunch.

I tried to talk them out of it, but no, they wanted to try one more time with a bigger piece of pipe. "I don't think we should," I said. "It's gonna go a long way. What if we hit something?"

Ignoring me, they propped up that big pipe with bricks and old boards in the middle of Seventh Street, pointed it toward D Hill and fired. Bricks and old boards scattered every which way. But we watched that smoking cylinder fly up Seventh Street past Estrella Avenue and disappear into The Desert. We rode our bikes up there, looked and looked, but never found it. Aw shucks, it was the last one we had.

I'm proud to tell you we never broke a window at the school. Nor did we do any other known damage. And most notable of all, we didn't shoot anybody's eye out.

It took us a week to advance from stage to stage in our rocketry because we had to wait until Doug's parents weren't home. However, when they weren't home, there were a bunch of breathless, sweaty angels running up and down Seventh Street.

"Folly is bound up in the heart of a child…"

—Proverbs 22:15

A Match Made in Agua Prieta

"I'd feel safer with my kids across the line at night than I would with them in Chicago in the daytime," I overheard Dad tell a friend. "Across the line" means Mexico, specifically Agua Prieta, Sonora, Mexico.

So, I went across the line a lot. I got all my haircuts there until I went into the Army. Fifty cents. I got my shoes repaired there ($3.00), bought sacks of bread rolls (50¢), bought a couple of baseball gloves (100 pesos, or $8.00), loaded up with firecrackers (5¢ for 100), plenty of cheap baseballs (25¢), many a trinket, *Chiclets* (2¢) and got my shoes shined once in a while for a dime.

"Honey, would you go get me some tomatoes and lettuce. Get a watermelon, too." Mom gave me a fifty-cent piece and I pedaled my bike to the Port. From there it was an easy walk to a vegetable stand behind the Mexican Customs Office. I bought Mom a half a sack of tomatoes, a head or two of lettuce, maybe a fat onion and a handful of long, fresh green beans. If it fit in the grocery sack, it only cost fifty cents. And I got a watermelon with it, too. Sometimes I talked her into an extra nickel and bought myself a Popsicle at *Mi Tienda*, a grocery store on the US side, just around the corner from the Port.

Avenida Internacional, Agua Prieta's main street, was concrete. Otherwise, most all the streets were dirt. Most of the homes were dirt, too. Adobe. Even the floors were dirt, and it was common to see Mexican housewives sweeping the dirt sidewalk in front of their screen doors.

Any chance I had to go across the line I took. I just liked it over there. I even went with the Fosters sometimes when they delivered firewood to their friends. That's where Doug learned to drive, by the way. He was about twelve or so when his dad let him drive us back to the US side. Mike, Jimmy and I rode in the back. Doug's dad took over when we got back to the Port. Our family took out-of-town visitors to get some tourist souvenirs and eat some real Mexican food. (My mom's was just as good.) Our friends felt safe with my dad, the Immigration Officer.

Dad and I went to Agua Prieta as often as anywhere else. The little town was just an extension of Douglas. We took loads of firewood over there year round. Dad always left behind a few fifty-cent pieces, too.

When I was in high school and worked at A.J. Bayless Grocery Store, a carload of us employees went to Agua Prieta after work for three big tacos and a bottle of beer. A great meal. Sixty-cent, including tip, and home by 10:00 p.m.

In US towns along the Mexican border, there are two more holidays to celebrate. Fine independence holidays, May 5 and September 16. September 16 has greater historical significance. May 5 is the more popular, (probably) because it's easier for English speaking people to pronounce: *Cinco de Mayo*.

From San Diego, California (Tijuana), to El Paso (Juarez) and Brownsville, Texas (Matamoros), US cities energetically join the Mexican fiestas to celebrate Independence and cultural kinship. Douglas and Agua Prieta do it, too.

The best May Pole dances were in Agua Prieta on *Cinco de Mayo*. Mexican May Poles were much taller and wider than Douglas ones. Many more children circled the poles while the Mexican bands played fine, brassy marches. One was always the color of the Mexican flag: red, white and green. The other was of dazzling bright ribbons of heavy yellows and greens and reds and dark blues and oranges and bright purples. Mexican people like their colors thick.

Diez y Seis de Septiembre, is one of my favorite holidays. *Free Food!* Mexican friends brought us tamales like it was Christmas. Dad gave them a little honey for their *sopapillas*. *Diez y Seis de Septiembre* is a good day. On that day in 1810, Father Miguel Hidalgo called for Mexico's freedom from Spain's oppression. It is the day that proud Mexican people began their bloody, ten-year fight for freedom. They did a good job.

There are other festivities in Agua Prieta, too. *"Vamos a plaza"* means "Let's go to plaza." Not "Let's go to *the* plaza." It means to walk around the plaza and check out the opposite sex.

Over in Agua Prieta is a little community plaza, or square, about a hundred feet on each side. A dry fountain sits in the center and dust swirls around in it on a windy day. A few trees struggle against the desert heat and somehow survive in the plaza. Several shops line up shoulder-to-shoulder across the narrow street. The surrounding cement sidewalk is two steps higher than the dirt street.

On weekend evenings, the plaza was the community. Handsome *vaqueros* (cowboys) came in from desert ranches. They stood tall in their clean boots and white palm cowboy hats, lining the dusty sidewalks, leaning against buildings, joking and smoking.

Pretty mothers and daughters came in their finest; their bright, black hair brushed and set. They were as pretty as Natalie Wood. Young boys put on their only clean shirt and scuffled around just like Anglo boys in Douglas. Local men wore their well-worn slacks and not-quite-clean dress shirts; sleeves rolled up. Single women in groups of three or four stayed closed to the shop doors until...

About dusk, the townspeople slowly walked the sidewalk around the plaza. The women walked one direction. Men, the opposite. While they circled, they flirted. People entered or exited the circles at any time. No loud talking.

Handsome, single *caballeros* (gentlemen) and the smoking *vaqueros* winked at the pretty girls as they passed each other. The girls coyly smiled back. Their mothers, pretending not to notice, moved their daughters forward around and around the plaza. The night was young. There was plenty of time to find a good man.

When a man spied the girl or woman of his dreams, he offered her a pretty white handkerchief as they passed each other. When they met again on the other side of the plaza, he looked to see if she still had the hanky. If she didn't have it, she wasn't interested in him. They both walked on. If she kept it, a match was made.

It didn't matter if the good man was Anglo, Indian, Black or Mexican. (There were no Asians around there.) It didn't matter if the pretty girl was barely in her teens or if she was *una cotorra* of twenty-five (something like a spinster). I do not know where they went after the match was made. Now, it may not have been a permanent match, so both probably showed up again on another weekend.

This old custom was common in small Mexican towns. *Touristas* won't see it when they visit the big cities like Juarez, Monterrey or Guadalajara. There's just too many people in the bigger towns. Besides, those big towns cater to busy American-style night life.

I walked the plaza only two times, probably when I was in intermediate school. I gawked at many a beautiful Mexican maiden. Many of them smiled at me. *Right at me!* Pretty smiles always made the back of my knees feel funny. It's a good thing Dad was there to catch me or I might have wobbled right off the sidewalk.

¡Viva Mexico! God bless Mexico, too.

• • •

Changing Times Department: Agua Prieta is a big city now with more than 120,000 people. No one goes *to plaza* anymore.

• • •

"...love your neighbor as yourself."

—Leviticus 19:18 and Mark 12:31

Border Wars

The US-Mexico border slices straight through Douglas and Agua Prieta. You can straddle the line with a foot in Mexico and a foot in the US. The foot in Mexico is poor and famished. The foot in the US is prosperous and flabby. The foot in Agua Prieta aches for one more step to freely cross the line. The foot in Douglas crosses the line and hurries back to thick burgers and cool sheets on the bed.

In the '50s, the two towns/countries were separated by a chain link fence, about 3/16 of an inch thick and twelve feet high. Three strands of barbed wire (bob waar) ran along the top. When I was little I asked my parents why that fence was there. I still haven't received a satisfactory answer.

We Seventh Street kids left our neighborhood several times and ended up at the fence, where before long some curious boys from Mexico wandered over. Sometimes one of us slipped Bazooka bubble gum through the fence to them. In return, they threw delicious, hard chunks of *piloncillo*, (dark brown sugar) over the fence and we sucked it like candy. I played catch with a taped-up baseball one time. I wanted to throw back and forth a little longer, but the Mexican boy turned and walked away with my old baseball. I threw a big dirt clod over the fence at him. Missed him.

We threw a lot of rocks and dirt clods at each other, especially when no one brought any sweets to exchange. We had some fierce and futile border wars. No one ever got hurt. It's easy to watch the rocks go up, then step to one side when they come down. Pick them up and throw them back. Generally, our wars were no more than shouting matches and name-calling. When we all saw how futile our efforts were, we got bored and sauntered off in opposite directions.

Wouldn't it be nice if politicians did something along the same lines?

We in America wandered back to our fun and games. The boys in Mexico went to work in the hot sun to earn a few *centavos*.

For the most part, we got along with the boys across the line. They're no different than anybody else. In broken English, they asked us for "fife senzz" or "Hairchie Bars" or "wan peeny." In worse Spanish, we shrugged our shoulders and told them, "*No tenemos.*" ("We don't have any.") If I knew I'd be near the fence, I tried to take along a few pennies. That's about the best I could do.

Doug Foster and I were out riding horses and hunting rabbits together. We were riding along on the Border Patrol road, outside the city limits near White Water Creek. We spotted a group of boys over in a Mexican lettuce field. They spotted us, too, and the shouting and name-calling began. *They started it first!*

Rocks arrived. One hit too close to Doug's horse. "Hold your reins tight," he said to me. He turned his rifle in the direction of those Mexican boys and fired. Too low, I thought. The Mexicans hit the dirt and dashed behind some scrub. From there they hurled some well-justified curses.

"You shouldn't have done that," I said. "What if you'd hit somebody?"

"So what?" he said back, still staring into Mexico.

"You know what what," I told him.

"Who they gonna tell?" he wanted to know.

We went on our way at a trot. Spanish curses, rocks and obscenities followed us for half a mile.

"*¡Gringos locos!*" We took a different route home.

I got worried. What if one or two of those boys recognized me at the Douglas Dump? What if they beat me up the next time they saw me there? What if they beat me up *again* and told me to give that beating to Doug? Ooh.

> *"And you are to love those who are aliens, for you yourselves*
> *were aliens in Egypt."*
>
> —Deuteronomy 10:19

Douglas Dump

"My goodness, son, go take a bath! Where on earth have you been? Take your clothes off outside and leave them on the back porch. And scrub the ring out of the tub when you're through!"

I just got back from the city dump, a trip I never wanted to miss. Get a whiff of that garbage! Stinky smelter smoke, road dust, burning tires and nearby stockyard manure blended nicely with that sour garbage. It wasn't just any old garbage odor. The Douglas city dump produced a world-class stench unmatched in the annals of methane gas.

(Someday I'd like to sit there again, take a deep breath and write a song I'll call "Feelin' Like Reelin'.")

When we arrived we were greeted by a horde of Mexican boys from across the line. They ranged from about age six to teens. They pounced on the pickup and unloaded almost before Dad stopped. Each boy got a penny or two. Older boys asked for an extra penny for the little ones with runny noses. If just one or two boys showed up they got nickels.

The dump wasn't the busiest place around Douglas, so the boys spent most of their day slogging through all the trash and garbage to pluck the smallest item of value. Their little piles of scrap metal, pop bottles, clothes and such were stashed under nearby mesquite bushes.

The boys were crusted with black soot and dirt. Most of them worked without hats or shirts and some wore no shoes. They smelled bad, too. I have no idea how or when they bathed. They all seemed high-spirited, happy and eager to help. At night they dragged their valuable, smelly scraps back home to Agua Prieta. Maybe they had as much as fifteen cents, too.

What were those boys doing in the US? Simple: they were daily illegal aliens. Where White Water Creek comes out of Mexico, there was a big hole under the border fence. (Maybe that's where they bathed—if there was any water in the creek.) The boys crossed under the fence and through the creek to help earn a living for their families.

Ironically, Dad had the full power of the US government to arrest those boys and send them back to Mexico. But why? Instead, he chatted with them and gave them a few coins and maybe a stick of Wrigley's Doublemint gum. They went home to Mexico every night, anyway.

The dump was a deep open pit that burned and smoldered twenty-four hours a day. Pollution? Environment? Recycle? Those were words not yet invented and silly ideas to boot.

Smoldering tires had their own black pile, and everything else burned wherever it fell. On any given day, six or eight fires consumed our garbage. Some rather large, others just a smoking heap.

"*Whomp!*" Every so often something exploded. "That sounded like a can of gasoline." Maybe it was only a jar, or it might have been a discarded bullet or an old car battery.

Dad always took a short, nonchalant walk along the edge of the pit looking for scrap lumber. If he spied some, the Mexican boys earned a couple of more pennies to help us load it. It went into our lumber pile or to Pastor Ybarra's house in Agua Prieta. I don't think we ever scavenged anything else out of there.

A man on a bulldozer was stationed out there. I never saw him do anything; he just sat under his big umbrella reading magazines that he had rescued. I think he was supposed to cover up ashes after a while.

Rats and cats prowled the dump. You might be surprised at which chased what. I liked going out there with the Fosters. Mr. Foster—Chet to all of us—let us take our .22s along. We shot at the rats and at hundreds of bottles. Mike Foster claimed he shot a rat once, but I doubt it. The dirty, furtive things were quick and shifty. There were not too many snakes out there. I guess because the man on the bulldozer moved the dirt around so much that the snakes never had a place to settle. Or maybe they were afraid of the rats.

One summer Dad and I went out there an unusual number of times—maybe four. On the first trip I happened to have two baseball gloves safely tucked away in the cab. One was the worst glove in the history of Douglas. The frazzled web just dangled, most of the laces were long gone or knotted up pretty good. Fingers flopped and the padding oozed out many games ago. It was evening and Dad was jabbering away with a man who was out there. I got my gloves and a ball and played catch with the last boy out there. I think his name was Enrique. He learned to say "play catch" in English. I learned *"tirale mi"* ("throw it to me").

Enrique proudly slipped on the beat up glove and pounded the pocket a couple of times. He adjusted the fingers, tugged on the loose laces, pounded the pocket some more and said, "Okay, *play cesh. Tirale.*" The first toss went right through the glove. Enrique tugged and tucked and before long he had the old glove in decent catching order.

When it was time to go, Enrique reluctantly returned my worthless glove. He never took his eyes off it. He stood close to my door till we drove away, leaving me to remember his desperate ache for something so simple.

Why didn't I give him that glove? I had no use for it. I was probably going to throw it away anyway. I felt bad, selfish. I promised myself that when we returned to the dump again, I'd give that old glove to Enrique. He was industrious enough to put it back together. I was about to perform a good deed and I felt great.

I took it the next trip, and the ones after that, too, but apparently Enrique was no longer in business there.

• • •

Changing Times Department: The old city dump is an organized, smoke-free, environmentally safe landfill now. There's no hole under the fence anymore.

• • •

"He who is kind to the poor lends to the Lord, and he will reward him for what he has done."

—Proverbs 19:17

Rainy Days

One of the sweet pleasures of desert life is sitting on the front porch during a summer rain.

Yes, it rained in Douglas every once in awhile. Two or three times a year, we got a full day's cloud cover with cool, refreshing, gentle rain. If we were lucky, one of those days was in the summer.

The rain settled people down. The nerve-wracked, the neurotics, the schitzos, the depressed, the bi-polars—we all slipped out onto our front porches during a good rain. Dust settled. The air cooled. Douglas smelled fresh and clean. Brothers liked their sisters and parents relaxed some chores. Kids stuck their tongues out to catch a sweet drop or two. *Mmmm!* Neighbors waved neighborly to each other.

"Hi there! Isn't this *nice?*"

"It's *lovely!* We sure do need it, don't we?"

On a cloudy, day-long rainy day the neighborhood boys gathered on Doug Foster's front porch. His mom (Eleanor to all of us) was awfully nice to let us hang out there and make all kinds of racket. Most of the girls drifted to the Haro's house or over to Lolita Barret's front porch.

We boys became experts at Canasta. Whenever Mike or Jimmy Foster got beat, they'd whine, accuse everyone of cheating, throw a temper tantrum and go do something else. We were glad to be rid of them—they cheated. Doug was always the winner at Canasta.

When we got bored playing with two decks, we added two more. We made some canastas in a hurry that way. When that got boring, we changed to Poker. We played just for playing. We never had any money, so we used matches or "Pick-up Sticks."

One rainy afternoon, we had a great game of matchstick poker going at Armando's house. There were about six of us and I was doing great. I had a big pile of matchsticks. Eventually the rain let up and Mom blew her whistle, which meant I had to go home.

I scooted my chair back slowly, hesitant to get up. "Aw, what can they do to me?" I dramatically threw down the extra cards I had.

"Hey! You're cheating!" I bolted out the door, across the muddy yard and down the sidewalk to our muddy yard.

They chased me all the way, which worried Mom but made a good laugh for the rest of us. Of course, the other players had their own stashes, they just hadn't found a sneaky way to dump them yet. Armando Contreras and Richie Verdugo were always the big winners at Poker.

Other rainy day activities included hide-and-seek indoors. We played in the house where the parents weren't home. We played in our house one day and it took me two hours to unransack it before Mom came home. If she had seen that mess…

At home, puzzles were a common pastime. I built plastic models and rainy days were perfect. The coffee table was always loaded with *Arizona Highways*, one of the dreamiest magazines ever produced, so I dreamt my way all over the state.

Ruth and I got out our set of 78 rpm "Bozo the Clown" records. Along with the records was an illustrated read-along book. A little bell cued us to turn each page. When Bozo got himself into helpless fixes, he'd yell for our help. *"Turn the page!* (Glub-glub) *Please hurry! Turn the page!* (Glub-glub) *Turn the page now!"*

Terrified with suspense, we held on for dear life, hoping and praying for the bell. "Bing." We were so relieved when Bozo got out of his fix on the next page. This set was not only good for rainy days, but for wintertime evenings, too. Ruth and I were careful to keep the four 78s from too many scratches and over the years we rescued Bozo many times.

There's a trick to reading on a rainy day. We went out into our musty middle shed and dove into the pile of old magazines. *The Saturday Evening Post, Look, Life, National Geographic, Gleanings in Bee Culture, Boy's Life, Arizona Highways.* Or we chose from plenty of books, too. Dad had volumes of classic poetry, some *Old Farmer's Almanacs*, lots of "Golden Books," which were read time and again by Ruth and me. After lunch it didn't take long to read ourselves to sleep.

Sometimes, I got in some piano practice—sometimes, even voluntarily. I told you rainy days affected us.

Those "heat holidays" were different from the hot days that produced vicious four o'clock thunderstorms. Those noisy storms lumbered through Douglas in about thirty minutes, leaving a tenth of an inch of rain in their wake.

We never had to clean the bathtub or do dishes during a lightning storm. *Yee-haw!* Mom was terrified of lightning storms. When one approached she ran around the house unplugging every possible electrical cord except one lone lamp. The radio, the deep fryer, clocks, the refrigerator, table lamps, you name it. After the storm passed she plugged everything in again.

After a big rainstorm, we hurried outside and sailed little chunks of wood in the street runoff and called it boat racing. We built dams, too. That is, we scooped dirt over the curb to hold back whatever water was still running down the street. I don't know why, we just did. It was always fun to race our bikes through standing water and try to splash the girls who were making mud pies.

Our parents didn't like us playing in the muddy rainwater because that's where polio came from, they said.

At the end of the street, under the sidewalk at A Avenue and Seventh Street, was the gutter drain. It was dirty, dangerous, open and unprotected. I crawled into that drain many, many times. I was usually chasing a ball that got away. It was a damp tunnel that always smelled like a sour dishrag. It was twenty degrees cooler in there than up on the sidewalk, maybe more. A lot of pipes criss-crossed down there, and frogs hip-hopped. I never saw any vermin, but I suppose rats, mice and snakes had homes in there somewhere. Boys up to about age ten walked upright inside that drain. Occasionally, we crawled in on our tummies, stood up and walked to Sixth Street. We emerged by Joe Pinedo's house. As cool as the drain was, we rarely played in there. Maybe it was a little too dark or smelly or narrow, or maybe the fear of polio kept us out. Our parents warned us that dirty, muddy water caused polio.

• • •

Little Boys Department: Puddles were created for little boys to stomp in. I've seen boys detour thirty feet out of their way just to splat one foot in a mud puddle. I never saw a girl do it.

• • •

*"The desert and the parched land will be glad;
the wilderness will rejoice and blossom."*

—Isaiah 35:1

Polio in Douglas

Polio scared our parents like cancer or missing children terrifies parents today. No one knew who it would strike. Or why. For one stricken child, whole families went reeling, emotionally and financially. But Americans could help.

Every school year we were given a thick card with twenty slots in it. Teachers showed us how to slide a dime into each slot. A week or two later, we returned the dime-laden card. It was okay if the card wasn't full. Every dime helped. We all understood that some people just didn't have that many dimes to spare, not even after two weeks.

The original "March of Dimes" fought polio. And guess what? A comedian, Eddie Cantor, coined the phrase.

The polio virus attacked children's nerves in their brain and spinal cord, often paralyzing them from head to toe. They had to live—lying down all the time—in iron lungs; huge, ugly contraptions that somehow helped the paralyzed lungs to work. Only the kid's head poked out from that terrifying iron lung.

My brother Neal had polio for a while before I was born, but he didn't have to live in the iron lung. Whew. I don't know how he overcame it and neither does he. I don't know of anyone in Douglas who had polio bad enough to be sent to Tucson to live in an iron lung. Oh, the very thought of it!

When I was in the fourth grade, the **Salk Vaccine** was introduced to the world. *It worked!* Almost every child in America was given this polio vaccine. My first polio vaccine was a sugar cube with some red stuff squirted on it. I ate it, as did my school chums, and that was that. For a few years after that, we got some sort of a booster. It was always at school and it was always free. The method of giving it to us was always different until it finally advanced to shots. I got my last polio shot when I was in the Army. It was a marvelous and miraculous medicine that saved the youth of uncounted children.

Our parents—all our parents—spoke so gratefully when they talked with their friends about this wonder drug. But they still didn't like us playing in the rainwater.

"Shout for joy...burst into song...For the Lord comforts his people and will have compassion on his afflicted ones."

—Isaiah 49:13

You Know Why They Shoot Horses, Don't You?

A block up from 1122 is Clawson School where I attended grades K to 4. I went there to learn, and indeed, I learned three fundamental things. But that's not the only reason I went there. I also went there to play football and baseball.

We played football games on the grassy side of Clawson. A dozen guys of several ages was about the maximum. We knocked each other silly for an hour or so. Various players came and went. We took turns hurting each other's feelings and pretty soon somebody got into a fight. Or maybe we got mad and stomped home. Amazingly, we always played tackle, but no one was ever injured. We spent a lot of time passing and punting and devising nameless contests with those skills.

We had two baseball diamonds. On the grassy side (Seventh Street side), it was our sole purpose in life to hit the ball up on the roof. Win or lose, if you hit the ball on the roof, it was a homer, the game was over and you were a big shot for about thirty minutes till someone found another baseball.

Every once in awhile we found three or four baseballs on the ground and we knew that maintenance people had been up on the roof and dropped them down for us. We appreciated that, but sometimes we knew they had sat in some rain water for awhile.

I was thirteen when I hit my only homer on the roof. It was a clean, solid, rising line drive. It felt good. There's no place like home plate.

Games on the grassy side were on a smaller diamond, smaller than softball size. Therefore, we rarely kept score, because scores usually ran up into the twenties and thirties. We didn't care who won, because we'd choose up sides differently the next time anyway.

Every time Jimmy Foster hit the ball, he knocked his cap off when he rounded first. Just like the big leaguers, his cap went a-flying in the wind. "Hah! You're not that fast, Jimmy. We saw you knock your hat off—again."

Games on the dirt side (Sixth Street side) were on a regulation size infield, a short outfield. When we played there, it was a serious and major event, with umpires and base coaches. About twice a summer, the Mexican boys from around First, Second and Third Streets—we called them "The First Street Gang"—rode their bikes over for a full nine inning game.

We rounded up all the guys from our neighborhood and from other neighborhoods within bike-riding distance.

The game was on. Sometimes even neighborhood adults leaned on the fence and watched us. Those were great games; well organized, honest, and fiercely fought. We played them in the heat of the desert sun from about 10 a.m. till noon.

Sad to say that The First Street Gang won more than we did, but when we did win, it was a big deal for us. They were *good*—and so *big*. They probably weren't any bigger than we were, we just didn't know them as well as we knew each other. After the game, we usually traipsed over to Early's Market for something cold to drink. If we didn't have a dime, we drank cool water out of the Foster's front yard faucet.

One Saturday a bunch of Mexican boys from Pirtleville answered our challenge for a game on the dirt side of Clawson. We recruited a few guys from The First Street Gang, as well as Joe Scarpignatto and Bobby Page for our team.

Pirtleville is a little town just outside Douglas. It's noted for two things. First, it has the only cemetery in the US (or used to anyway) where the graves face south—toward Mexico. Second, it was once pin-pointed in a 1950s *Saturday Evening Post* feature called "Where in the World Are You?"

Those "boys" from Pirtleville were men and high school guys. They came in cars and pickups and brought six brand new baseballs. They wore spikes and matching red caps. I only batted once, but I did catch a fly ball in left—all the way back on the grassy side of Clawson. Alas, we struck out 27 consecutive times. They used a different pitcher every inning. They didn't want to play us anymore.

I learned three things at Clawson School. Two involved George Sabin, who spent two years in the first grade and almost two years in the second grade.

Clawson School has four hallways, thus it's shaped like a plus sign. A central assembly area joined the four hallways. If an unusually loud noise came from that area, it was heard up and down all four hallways.

Mr. Elliott, our principal, took George Sabin in there one day and spanked him with that paddle he hung on his wall. George wailed unusually loud. Up and down all four hallways the other students were unusually quiet. That day I learned that I never wanted to make a trip to the Clawson School principal's office.

When the second grade was almost over, Miss Shrum told us solemnly that George Sabin drowned in the city pool last night. He got in by climbing over the chain-link fence. George is the only student I know of who died during my years in the Douglas school system. At Clawson school, of all places, I learned that it's important to know how to swim as early in life as possible.

One afternoon up at Clawson School while waiting my turn to bat I absent-mindedly turned a scuffed, dirty, warped baseball in my hand. I almost made out the words "Genuine Horsehide." It occurred to me that God created horses just so we'd have baseballs. It also occurred to me that people are born with *two* hands for the sole purpose of catching baseballs. I learned to love baseball up at Clawson School.

"Be happy, young man, while you are young, and let your heart give you joy in the days of your youth..."

—Ecclesiastes 11:9

The Last Batter

I was five years old when Neal solemnly took me into the bedroom one August evening, sat me down on the edge of Dad's bed and as gently as possible broke the news to me.

"Babe Ruth died today," he said.

"Who's she?" I asked.

I think he rolled his eyes and said things like "Home Run King" and "New York Yankees." I became a Yankee fan that night (because it was the only team I knew about) and began my baseball career the next day.

There was no such thing as T-ball when I grew up, so I learned to bat by tossing the ball in the air and swinging at it when it came down. If I didn't have a ball, I used rocks, which ruined my wooden bats. I smacked Noel's bean bag, too, when he wasn't looking. I taught myself to catch grounders out in the street. I threw a baseball, or a tennis ball, or a golf ball against the curb and caught it when it rebounded. I hung an old tire on the garage door and pitched myself to exhaustion in the Neatest Driveway on Earth. I developed a serious addiction to radio broadcasts of the World Series, sponsored by Gillette.

"To look sharp, da-da-da-da-dah; to feel sharp, da-da-da-da-dah; to BEEE sharp, use Gillette Blue Blades, for the quickest, slickest shave of all."

It only took two boys to get a baseball game going in a vacant lot. Pretty soon, another boy or two showed up. Sandlot baseball was a way of life for us. My older brothers didn't play with us very often, but all the boys my age played almost every summer day—and almost all of the Saturday mornings, too. If we weren't in a vacant lot, we were up at Clawson School. I never liked to stop—especially when Mom blew her dumb whistle.

I was ten or eleven when Noel became my hero. My brother—*my brother!*—was the visiting team batboy in Douglas' Class C minor league ball park. Can you believe it? My brother—*my* brother!—had an official uniform, got in the game free and got to sit in the dugout with professional baseball players! They even let him keep the broken bats. He got an autographed baseball signed by all the players on the team. From time to time he brought me an almost clean baseball. Noel was *it!* and life was good.

Douglas and Bisbee shared a minor league affiliate of the Pittsburgh Pirates. The Bisbee-Douglas Copper Kings of the Class C Arizona-Mexico League. They played a few games in Douglas, then a few games in Bisbee against teams from Mexicali, Cananea, El Paso, Phoenix and Tucson. Different teams came and went. Globe-Miami, Nogales, Juarez. Douglas provided a really nice stadium for teams and fans alike. For a dime, we sat in the "Knot Hole Section" in the third base bleachers.

Every year, Douglas hosted one Spring Training game between the Pittsburg Pirates and somebody else. Fans from all over Cochise County jam-packed the stadium. The sun was bright. If kids didn't get in, they hung over the outfield fence and watched from there. One year the Giants came to town and Douglas got to see Willie Mays for a couple of innings.

There were several years when the Yankees asked me to pinch hit in the bottom of the ninth of the Seventh Game of the World Series. They were always in a two-out jam and three runs behind. I always stepped up to the plate in front of that roaring crowd and promptly pounded a grand slam deep into Yankee Stadium's upper deck. Year after year Mickey Mantle, Gil McDougal, Phil Rizzuto, Yogi Berra, Enos Slaughter, Hank Bauer, Bobby Richardson, Billy Martin, Whitey Ford and all the rest of them gleefully carried me off on their shoulders! The roaring, frenzied crowd...

• • •

Back to Reality Department: Hey, gimme a break. It's every American boy's Number One Dream.

• • •

120

• • •

When I was nine, I was drafted onto the Elks Little League farm team. I was disappointed that I didn't get on a team with a complete uniform, but I got a blue T-shirt that said "B. P. O. E." I got a blue cap with "E" on it. I rode my bike—or walked—to every game or practice, and our team won all our games. Jack Murray, a Douglas policeman, was our coach and teacher.

The next year I was disappointed again that I was not picked for a "major league" team. But I slipped my glove over my handlebars and rode off to all our games. I still had my blue T-shirt. I was the star pitcher for Elks (farm team), and we won all our games again. Mr. Murray was still our coach. He invited us over to his front porch after the games to glug all the Kool-aid we wanted. Life was good.

Finally, when I was eleven I was drafted onto "Fair's Sporting Goods" team. Mr. Garcia gave me my white and green uniform. My chest puffed up really good when I turned my jersey around and saw the number 1. Last year, Fairs was the intimidating team to beat. They finished in first place and had three or four guys on the All-Star team. Would we live up to that high standard? Mr. Garcia said we would—or else!

I went to bat thirty-nine times that year. I walked five times. I struck out thirty-three times. I was always the last batter. I hated it when some otherwise nice lady up in the bleachers hooted, "Easy out! He can't hit!" I really was a good batter. Everybody knew that. "Just roll it. He'll miss it! Easy out!" But why couldn't I hit this year? "Struck him out again! Ha! Ha! Ha!"

My one and only hit came with one game left in our Little League season, a bloop single over second base. Joe Scarpignato teased me for two years. "Strikeout King" and "One Hit Nichols." I always replied, "I got it off you!"

Well, we didn't live up to that high standard. It was a miserable year. First, I struck out all the time, essentially giving our team only two outs per inning. Second, there were only ten boys on our team. If two didn't show up, we had to commandeer someone in street clothes to play right field. That's against Little League rules. And third, the others teams were flat-out better than us.

Fairs Little League team. Dad took this picture. I am kneeling front row, far left.

The next year, my first hit—my first at bat—was a line drive double against Joe Scarpignato. Down the third base line it zang, all the way to the fence. Joe just laughed and said, "That's your one hit for this year, Nichols." He was wrong. I batted about average that year. Defensively, I was out standing in my field. I stood out in the outfield, where I made some magnificent catches and threw out a few runners. I committed no errors that year. It was fun. Life was good.

In our first game of Babe Ruth Baseball (age 13), Joe taunted me from the pitcher's mound. "I'm going to hit you, Nichols!" He used a mocking, exaggerated windup and threw me a great slow strike. It was pretty, but I let it pass. I let the next one pass, too. I figured his windup would settle down and his last pitch would come flying straight through the strike zone about a hundred miles an hour. I was about to shut him up for good. He settled down alright, but another slow pitch came arcing to the plate. I swung too early.

"You're *still* the strikeout king! How many is that in your career, One Hit?"

Joe was a good all-around athlete, a good baseball player and a good pitcher. A handsome teenager with girls dripping off him no matter where he was, Joe and I got along pretty good when we weren't playing baseball. He spoke good Spanish, too, so I was never really sure if he was an Italian or a Mexican. Maybe he was both.

Our Babe Ruth field, hidden behind the gym, was also the high school varsity practice field. It's an impressive, well-cared-for field that a lot of other cities would show off on main street. The outfield fence is 300 feet all the way around. I promise you there is no greater feeling than ripping one over the left field fence. I did it twice.

We were fifteen years old and Joe Scarpignato threw me an ugly high curve ball way out of the strike zone. But I swung, anyway. Luckily, I hit it and drove it ten feet over the fence. Not so luckily, it was foul all the way. Of course, it wasn't a hit, but it went over the fence, didn't it? All I had to do now was keep it fair.

A couple of games later, I batted four times. Each time, I hit the ball into left field. My first three fly balls were caught, each a little deeper in the field. My fourth at bat...I can still see the sweet part of the bat coming around to meet the ball. I can still hear the sound of it, too. It's the perfect sound. That ball was long gone, over the fence and lost in the tumbleweeds. Life was good.

I promise you: even when you're the last batter, there's no place like home...plate.

"A heart at peace gives life to the body..."

—Proverbs 14:30

The Good, The Bad and The Ugly

The Nichols kids were not allowed to date Mexican kids. Period.

The first girl I ever kissed was Roxanne Somebody, a girl in my first grade class. Some of my hormones went haywire one day and I ran up and kissed her on the cheek, then ran away. She tattled to Miss Halliday, who told me, in front of the whole class, not to kiss the girls. How embarrassing!

My first date ever was with Shelly Rose Harris when we were in the fifth grade. I called her on the phone (with my mother's blessing) and formally asked her out.

Doug Foster said, "Her? You're crazy, man. She's got a big honky nose."

Shelly Rose and I walked to a Saturday afternoon matinee at the Grand Theatre and sat in the balcony. Friends, both hers and mine, giggled past to see if we were holding hands. We were. After the movie, we took the long way home.

Betty Hooper was sort of forced upon me about the same time. For some reason, our moms thought we'd make a fine couple. We went to church together and Sundays were the only days I saw her. She was a year younger. For several Sundays, Betty managed to muscle her way next to me, not caring at all who saw us. My Sunday School friends snickered at us and teased me at school, too.

"Her? Paul, you're crazy," they said. "Betty's ugly." I never really liked her.

When Christmas rolled around that year Mom made me spend one of my dollars on a box of stationery for Betty. Mom wrapped it nicely and we took it over to the Hooper's. That was the only time I went to her house. Betty was doing the dishes or something, so her mother, an overweight woman who had no smile, accepted the gift on her behalf and abruptly shut the door. "That's funny," I thought. I walked back to the car without even a "thank you."

"What did she say?" Mom asked me, referring to Betty.

"Her mom took it," I said.

"That figures."

"That's funny," I thought.

The morning before Christmas, Betty's mom brought her to my house. She gave me an enormous present, wildly wrapped with layers and layers of the *Douglas Daily Dispatch*. It was three times bigger than a basketball and held together with green yarn.

"Oooh. What's this?" I pressed it; I shook it; I held it to my ear. What is it? And so light! Betty hurried back to the car before I had a chance to say "thank you." "Wow! I've never had a present this big," I marveled. I even smelled it. Wait until we open presents? I'll never make it.

"She must have spent a lot if it's this big," I said to myself. "I hope she likes what I got her. I only spent a dollar."

That afternoon I called her and begged her to tell me what it was, but she wouldn't. Then I got the bright idea that we both open our gifts right now. "Okay," she said, "but I have to hang up now."

I tore into that bundle of newspapers, ripping, pulling and scattering until finally there I found it: my new Christmas paddle and ball.

"A paddle and ball! I've got three of them already! She only spent a dime!? And look at all this newspaper!" I rummaged through the paper in case I missed a dollar bill or something. "Is that all? Just a paddle and ball! That's for little kids! She only spent a dime! And she didn't even use a real ribbon!"

I huffed and puffed and stomped outside. I flang that paddle down Seventh Street all the way across A Avenue. The last I saw of it, it was skittering along the curb in front of the Valenzuela's house. Betty Hooper ruined my Christmas.

Besides that, she never did send me a thank you note for the nice stationery I gave her. I decided not to like her at all, and ignored her at every opportunity. I promised myself to see no more of her!

Sarah Marley School was somewhat special to Douglas because just before my age group started school, Sarah Marley was called 7th Street School and only Mexican students attended there. It was integrated in 1946 or '47 and the name was changed. However, few, if any, Anglo students attended there while I was growing up on Seventh Street.

Back in the third grade, our class visited Sarah Marley School, about six blocks down Seventh Street. We walked. We visited the two third grade classes, which were full of Mexican kids. We lined up around the walls until we all fit in.

I spied a pretty Mexican girl in the middle of that first room. She had great big, friendly eyes—and she spied me, too. So I got great big, friendly eyes. We timidly smiled at each other and from that moment on I liked Gloria Amaya. It took me three more years to learn her name. I always thought we were special friends. Good friends.

Over the years, Gloria and I crossed dusty paths several times. We always took a big, friendly look at each other. I'll bet we never said ten words to each other until eventually we shared a classroom in high school. We got to sit next to each other in typing class. Gloria played in the band, so sitting next to each other during football games was out.

A time or two, Gloria and I met at a movie or something and I called that a date. We danced at the sock hop after the games. I accepted a spontaneous invitation to eat in her home once. We made sure we shared the same seat on a school bus trip back from Tucson one night. I think I broke her heart that night, not long before our graduation. I was conflicted about being right there next to her and yet hearing the voices of my parents ringing in my conscience: "*No, you are not allowed to date Mexican kids.*" But why not? It was such a painful dilemma that as soon as the bus arrived back in Douglas I got off—a full mile from our house—and walked home. I think I broke my own heart that night, too. I always had a hard time working out those kinds of things. Do you think I told any of this to my parents? Maybe I should have.

If she were an Anglo girl, Mom and Dad would have trumpeted us all over town. Gloria was a **good** person from a **good**, hard-working Presbyterian family. But because she was a Mexican girl, all reason went out the window. The Nichols kids were not allowed to date Mexican kids. Period. That was a **bad** deal.

126

Wouldn't you know it? In my eighth grade year Betty Hooper raised her ugly head again. She stole someone's wedding rings.

On a hot spring day she was arrested during lunch hour, caddy-corner from the junior high school, in sight of plenty of curious kids and her obese mother. I was outside on the gymnasium steps when we saw her bolt off the front porch of the home across the street. Her narrow little arms handcuffed in front of her, she hurried to the police car five steps ahead of the officer and flung herself into the back seat. Her huffing, puffing mother waddled down the porch steps, screaming things we couldn't quite hear. Mrs. Hooper jabbed a sinister fat finger through the car window. Her frightened little girl tried to cover her ears. She fell onto the seat, out of our final view.

The officer drove off toward the police station. Mrs. Hooper drove off in the other direction. Betty was seen no more in Douglas. Her parents didn't see her no more, too. They didn't want her no more. They didn't speak of her no more. A little girl was completely no more. Like a water drop on the desert floor.

That evening, while rumors blazed through Douglas, I gleefully eavesdropped on Mom's phone conversations. "...cruel parents..." "...spoiled brother..." "...not the first time she took something."

"Yes, the same Hoopers that go to our church..."

The same Hooper's that went to our church mistreated their daughter. They neglected her and rejected her in her own home. The Hoopers practiced child abuse on Betty thirty-five years before I ever knew there was such a thing.

Betty and her younger brother Joey were adopted. Cinderella? I think so. She did all the chores; Joey none. My sister Ruth was at her house once and Betty was polishing shoes. *All the family shoes!*

Joey received privileges that Betty didn't. Mommy drove him to and from school every day. Betty walked. A strict daily work regimen was forced upon Betty while Joey leisurely read comic books. Betty was soundly punished for the most minor infractions; Joey not at all.

Despite doing everything, Betty only wanted one thing: a little love. Apparently that's what she got: and very little.

She was taken away, but I still didn't like her. That stupid Christmas present was still on my mind.

I went back to school thinking that maybe Betty was ugly because she lived in an **ugly** home. Or maybe because she was snatched up by people with **ugly** ideas. Or perhaps because she had to endure all that **ugly** torment. If I see her in heaven, I'm sure she'll be as pretty as Cinderella.

"I will save you from the hands of the wicked and redeem you from the grasp of the cruel."

—Jeremiah 15:21

The Fifth Greatest Day
in the
History of the World

A piano is a grand thing. I enjoy piano music. I admire good pianists. I enjoy Mozart, Beethoven (the guys who thought outside the box) and all their contemporaries. I like Jerry Lee Lewis and Billy Joel. I appreciate the faithful pianists who play at church week after week after week. Some of them are really talented. I especially enjoy black pianists. Did you know they don't play with their fingers? They play with their souls.

In the meantime, I enjoy just about any kind of music you can throw at me. Among my many trials and errors there is a piano, a trombone, and the tenor section. Let's face it: I enjoy listening, not performing. I suppose it's something like standing in an art museum and looking.

Now a piano *lesson*—that's a key of a different stroke.

The reason piano lessons are bad is because you have to do them before you can play baseball. Worse yet, you have to do them while your friends are already outside playing baseball.

Mom and Dad had great visions of me (and Ruth) playing in Carnegie Hall. So they made us take piano lessons. They didn't know what they had gotten into. I had enough whiny excuses to fill a fat notebook. After awhile I just whined by the number.

"Five. Oooh, Fiiiive!"

I think I know the two reasons why the piano and I never got along.

First, on the night before my first lesson (looking forward to it, by the way), I sat down to the piano and tried to play a little ditty. But where to begin? How to make it sound pretty? I had no clue. So I just clunked a few keys. I turned around to Mom looking for an encouraging word. She looked at me sternly and asked, "Is that the best you can do?" Whatever enthusiasm I had for my first lesson melted away. I just got up and walked off.

Second, at that time my brother Neal was my hero. He was off to a Navy reserve summer camp. He had a uniform and everything and was coming home that afternoon. What a great day! Not so. I was delivered to my first piano lesson while Dad got to go out to the airport to get Neal. *No fair!*

So this eight-year-old boy, his feelings hurt, sitting on a strange piano bench, in a strange teacher's home (Mrs. Freedman's); his mind at the airport, his heart longing for his hero, and his legs dreading the walk home in the hot August sun, just had no interest whatsoever in a piano that day. Nor in that lesson. Nor in the lessons that followed. Whenever I practiced the piano, I was always somewhere else.

I was forced to practice those piano lessons for five years. I don't say forced lightly. I dreaded practice times. To this day I can tell you to the second when thirty minutes has passed. How many arpeggios got interrupted when my thirty minutes were up?

Recitals are worse. Piano recitals are the perfect recipe for embarrassing young boys. My parents were proud of me, though, regardless of how many times I corrected myself during a recital piece.

I once embarrassed myself to no end at church. Pastor Cosby's family was invited to a recital one Sunday afternoon. They sat with my parents and afterwards suggested that I play something in church that evening.

"Practice!? Again? Aw, Mom," I whined. I spent the rest of the afternoon practicing a hymn to play that evening. I never got it right. I knew I wasn't ready to perform. I detected a disaster.

On our way to evening church my hands got clammy wet. In the pew they got clammier and clammier. My mouth dried up and my hair hurt. I think I was going blind. I hoped so, anyway.

Then the terrifying moment arrived. With great verbal fanfare, Pastor Cosby promised something wonderful. I *tried* to go blind. Somehow my wobbly knees held up long enough for me to collapse onto the piano stool. When I got there I fumbled around for the right page. Next, before I ever got started, the book slipped off its stand and crashed onto the keys. I heard my smirking friends on the back row. I finally began by missing the first note or two. I started over. I missed a lot of other notes and backed up to play them correctly.

"Maybe if I just stop here and play my recital piece," I reasoned. No, that wouldn't work. I'd already forgotten it.

"Maybe if I fell over sick…" That wouldn't work, either. Mom had ways of making us feel better real quick. I was feeling sick, though. Honest.

I played just one verse (twice, if you count all the backups) and slunk back to my seat. All was quiet, except for the "snork-snork" noises from the back row. No one ever asked me to play the piano in church again.

Not long after that, Mom told me I didn't have to take lessons anymore if I didn't want to. Next to my wedding day and my children's births, that was the greatest day in the history of the world.

• • •

Or was it? Department: One evening just before supper, when I a freshman or sophomore in high school, Mom leaned out the front door to ask if I'd like to attend a piano concert later that evening. Well, no. Didn't she see the ball and glove in my hands? The next day at school, a few of my friends were buzzing about the concert. I had just missed a fabulous performance by the great Van Cliburn.

• • •

"Sing to him a new song; play skillfully, and shout for joy…"

—Psalm 33:3

Dairy Queen Rides

It was a big deal when the Dairy Queen opened in Douglas at the corner of G Avenue and Fourteenth Street. It was a popular place for quite some time. Other than the two drug stores, it was the only place in town that sold ice cream cones. Cones. Big ones, too.

My dad developed the idea of a Dairy Queen Ride. We kids piled into the back seat of the car. Mom piled in the front and Dad drove us to the Dairy Queen. Everyone got a good-sized cone, and then we rode up to D Hill. Mom and Dad were in the front holding hands, I think. By the time we got home we'd finished the Dairy Queens, had trails of sticky melted ice cream down our arms, and were happily full. There were a dozen well-used napkins strewn about the back seat. All pant legs were spotted with drips, drips, drips.

Occasionally, I got a Dilly Bar, and once Dad let me get the biggest cone they had. It cost a quarter, it was as tall as my whole head, it melted fast and I slept good that night. I also liked the chocolate-dipped cones and played little games trying to get ice cream out without breaking the chocolate. Most of the time, though, something went wrong and I resorted to gobbling.

Dairy Queen rides were reserved for the night of a full moon. Always. Only. Sometimes the moon had already risen by the time we got to D Hill, but most often we'd get there and wait for the moon to slide up over the mountain. The moon was huge and full and bright enough to light up the whole county. It was a pretty sight. I swear there was a time or two I could have walked right up to that man-in-the-moon and pinched his cheek.

When a full moon was scheduled on Sunday, we went to evening church first. Those were the longest services ever. And sure enough, Mom or Dad ended up standing around chit-chatting till the moon was way up there.

But a Dairy Queen Ride was always a good time, and Ruth and I always looked forward to those special evenings. I think my mom did, too. Neal and Noel ate the fastest and then "helped" Ruth finish hers.

The only time we didn't go for a Dairy Queen Ride was on a cold winter night—but we wanted to.

Dairy Queen is good for little boys who just had their tonsils removed. "Dr. Duncan said you can have all the ice cream you want!"

On the evening after I had my six-year-old tonsils removed, I heard everyone in the kitchen enjoying a carton of Dairy Queen. Mom brought me a dish. I was feeling miserable and still smelled ether. I waved her off (the only time I ever turned down ice cream).

"Honey, it's ice cream. Daddy went and got you some Dairy Queen. Don't you want it?"

No.

I heard her go back to the kitchen and say, "He doesn't want his."

"Good," I heard Noel say.

But I was ready when the next Dairy Queen ride rolled around.

"These days should be remembered and observed in every generation by every family..."

—Esther 9:28

The Haunted House on Ninth Street

Douglas had a haunted house right across from Charlie Ables' house on the corner of Ninth Street and E Avenue.

A big, spooky house, painted dark gray, partially hidden by old trees and bushes, it's dark and gloomy, for sure. A high fence hid the back yard, and an imposing black wrought-iron fence circled the front yard.

I cautiously asked Charlie who lived there. "I don't know," he said. "I never see anybody."

They say no lights ever came on in that house. No people entered or exited. No visitors knocked on the door. No mail or milk was left on the porch. No sounds ever came out of the house.

Well, almost none.

Many years ago, the story goes, on the first night the house was occupied, a beautiful young widow was murdered there. I heard that it was a terribly noisy affair. The young lady fought to the bitter end. No one ever found her killer, who still wanders around Douglas looking for his next victim. It might be...*you!*

There's only one way to find out who the murderer is. If you're close to the house you might hear *"Aiieeaah! Eeeeeh!"* That's the eerie sound of the widow's ghost announcing that the murderer has just walked past!

They say it's such a terrifying sound that you can only turn and run away as fast as you can. Don't look to see who walked past—just run!

I never heard that eerie sound. But on dark nights when we told ghost stories in 10th Street Park, a few of my brothers' friends said they heard it. I'm sure they did. They repeated it so well that it made my hair stand straight up.

I'm thankful that in the daytime it was safe to walk past that haunted house. All was calm. Just to be on the safe side, though, I always walked on the other side of the street.

When I had my paper route, I rode past the haunted house every morning to throw a paper next door. I always hurried past.

"When I am afraid, I will trust in you."

—Psalm 56:3

Five in the Morning

I figure you're not an All-American boy if you never bagged groceries or had a paper route. I did both so I'm a real honest-to-goodness All-American boy. I used to be, anyway. My brother Noel was, too, for awhile. He delivered the morning *Arizona Republic*.

I delivered the *Tucson Daily Citizen*, an afternoon paper, while I was in middle and junior high schools. It was a small route with about thirty papers, which I picked up at Jack Murray's house every afternoon. I delivered them on my bike all over the south half of Douglas. I carried all my papers in a big canvas bag. I conveniently fit it over my handle bars or wore it over my shoulders. On Saturday mornings I collected the money. The whole time I delivered papers the price was $2.20 a month.

A couple of years was enough of the hot afternoon sun. When a route for the *Arizona Daily Star* opened up, I took it. Less hot mornings. That route had about sixty papers in the same part of town. Doug Foster had the other route. The *Star* was another Tucson paper. After I finished my route I sold ten papers in front of the Gadsden Hotel and across the street in front of the Pioneer Café. 10¢ each. I got to keep half that. I only did that a couple of months because Mom and Dad said it was adversely affecting my school work.

My morning route was a good one. Quite frequently, I crossed paths with Quentin Cabarga, the Shamrock Dairy milk man. He delivered milk to nearly every house in town. Milk came in wax-coated hard-paper cartons. His little green delivery truck had loud brakes that squealed door-to-door on every street. It's a wonder anybody in Douglas ever slept past five in the morning.

Quentin always gave me a quart of chocolate milk. I always offered a quarter to pay for it, but he always said, "It's okay. Don't worry about it." A few times he accepted my extra paper.

Funny thing, I often met up with Quentin pretty close to the Haunted House on Ninth Street. It didn't take long to conduct my transaction and get scootin', chug-a-luggin' my quart of chocolate milk.

Across the street from Sarah Marley School, I rode my bike past a house where a big brown dog waited on the porch for me. Every morning, Stupid chased me two blocks up the street, barking and nipping at my heels or handlebars. I never trusted that dog. Even though he never bit me there was a time or two I felt his teeth nip the heel of my shoe.

I finally got fed up with him. I bought some 54-inch leather shoelaces and braided three of them together. Now I had a whip, which I fastened to a piece of broomstick. It was a good one, too. I was about to teach Stupid a lesson.

Next morning I was up a little earlier and pedaled a little faster to get through my route. I slowed down when I approached the dog's yard. I got my whip ready. Sure enough, here he came a-barkin'.

I whipped out my whip and lashed that big ol' dog right between the eyes and over the top of his head. *What a hit! Perfect!* Stupid yelped and bolted back to the porch, still yelping when he got there.

The morning after that I was ready again. Here he came again. Not-So-Stupid stopped in the middle of his sidewalk and barked, barked, barked till I was a half a block up the street.

I carried my whip with me every day after that, but never used it again. But every morning, Not-So-Stupid ran to the middle of his sidewalk and barked, barked, barked till I was a half a block up the street. Poor neighbors. I wonder if anybody along the 700 block of Seventh Street ever slept past five in the morning.

When I was fourteen, Dad bought me a noisy, green Cushman Eagle motor scooter. No more pedaling my bike. It was a noisy thing, but it made a big difference in time and ease of delivery. It's a wonder anybody from the border to Ninth Street ever slept past five in the morning.

I didn't earn a lot of money from my routes, but enough for a few pinball games (5¢ each) school supplies, licorice sticks, baseballs, shirts of my choice, and a glove my dad talked me into buying. It was wide with short fingers. I wish I had gotten one with long fingers and a wide web. Better for playing first base or making shoe string catches in the outfield. Looking back, I think Dad wanted me to get the short-fingered one because it reminded him of his era's early-edition gloves.

On "payday," I almost always went to the Douglas Drug and ordered a hamburger, a cherry 7-Up and some fries. *Mmmm* Hamburger and bun, both done on a big, flat grill. The burger topped with fresh tomato, lettuce, pickles and onion. Fries piled high next to it. Friends across the booth. Friends in the next booth, too. All of us eating the same thing. All of us paid 55¢.

In the summer I made a special trip to the new Dairy Cream across from the high school. Tom Rodman worked there and if you said the magic words, he made shakes so thick that if you turned them upside down nothing fell out. 25¢.

●　●　●

Phoenix Newspaper Department: Even though I threw Tucson papers, and even though Tucson printed more Southern Arizona news items, my parents subscribed to the more sophisticated *Arizona Republic* from Phoenix. They faithfully read "Dunkin' with Duncan," a slice-of-life column by Arnott Duncan, our Dr. Duncan's son.

●　●　●

"Whatever you do, work at it with all your heart, as working for the Lord, not for men..."

—Colossians 3:23

Technicolors for Grandmother

Our Grandmother came from California every three or four years. She stayed six weeks. I never really knew her all that well. She was Dad's mom. After my grandfather passed away before I was born, she married a Mr. Marple. He died before I was born, too, and Grandmother remained a widow from then on.

Most of the time that I knew my grandmother, Amy Marple, she read books wearing three pair of hook-on glasses and used a magnifying glass, too. She eventually lost all her sight. When she visited, she brought a trunk full of Braille books and a Braille writer, a little hand-held stylus that she used to press dots into paper so she could read it. She always arrived on the train, the *Sunset Limited*.

Motley Crue, eat your heart out! Neal and Noel are behind me, Grandmother and Ruth. c1947

Because she was pretty old and pretty blind, we didn't do things that other grandparents and grandkids did. When Mom and Dad made us be nice to her, we just sat around the living room or front porch describing things to her. Grandmother always wanted us to tell her the color of something. The rest was just details.

"What color is their front door?"

"What color is your bike?"

"Ruthie, what color is this dolly's blanket?

I went to see *The Robe* one afternoon (Richard Burton, Jean Simmons and Victor Mature). When I got home, Grandmother asked me to tell her about the movie. I was ten. I sat down on the couch with her and recited it from beginning to end. It must have taken me thirty minutes to tell her the whole story, and she sat there carefully listening and interrupting.

"What color was the robe?"

"What color was her costume?"

"What color was his uniform?"

"Was that outdoors or indoors?"

"Did they have a window or did they use candles?"

"What did she say after that? Did she cry?"

I was her eyes for that movie, so I tried to be as vivid as I knew how. I wish I'd known she was going to test me. I would have paid more attention. Mom called us to dinner during my recalling, but Grandmother told her to go ahead and eat. We'd be there after I finished the story. Which I promptly did.

I wonder if that few minutes on the couch with Grandmother was the seed of my story-telling. Even though I didn't know her all that well, I always sent her "Thank you" notes after Christmas and my birthday.

Years and years ago, my grandmother was a missionary to the Comanche Indians near Fort Sill, Oklahoma. It's my understanding that she knew the great Comanche leader, Quanah Parker. It don't get much better than that.

Grandmother passed away in 1962 while I was in the Army.

• • •

Proud Moment Department: We named Amy after Grandmother, and after the beautiful sunrise that greeted her: Amy Dawn. Isn't that a pretty name? Mom told us that when Dad heard her name, he just about exploded with delight.

• • •

"I have been reminded of your sincere faith,
which first lived in your grandmother…"

—2 Timothy 1:5

Church Services on Seventh Street

We were pretty ornery boys when church services were held on Seventh Street. Mr. Early sold his grocery store, locked the doors and drove his family out of town. A little family moved into the attached apartment and soon opened a church in the cleaned-out store. That is, they opened up a place where their cult met.

And boy, did they ever meet! Every night they held services. Mama was the minister and wore a white gown when she led services. The teen-aged daughter also wore a white gown and stood on the low, empty podium near Mama. Papa wore gray slacks and a dirty, never-ironed shirt. Always. Day and night. He passed the money basket and sat down in the back during service. He seemed old to me. I never saw him go to work in the daytime.

I know what they wore and who did what because we just looked through the big plate glass windows and watched. Remember, it once was a store. I guess they passed the basket enough to finally buy some cheap curtains. We still saw right through them, though.

I never went into their "church." For a Baptist boy like me, it was an unnerving idea to go in there. Armando Contreras, John Matson and Luis Rodriguez attended a service one night and about twenty minutes after it started came out laughing.

The little church didn't last long there. It's all our fault, too. During services, we kids—boys and girls alike—belted out our best hollering and barked cat-calls at each other. As soon as the congregation settled in we played four-corners and kick-the-can. We inserted several pebbles into the cans.

Everybody wanted to be "it" just to kick the can anywhere we wanted. And we wanted to kick it right toward the church door. It took an unusually long time of noisy scuffling and rattling to get the can kicked away from there.

Papa—whatever his name was—came out in his dirty shirt and timidly asked us to play somewhere else. But we didn't.

At the end of services, the parishioners poured out the front door and walked away into the night. All six of them.

Well, pretty soon the little church quit having services. I don't know if it was because it didn't have very many followers, or if the boys and girls on Seventh Street made too much racket, or if they didn't get any tax breaks after all. The family moved to the Coronado Courts up on Eighteenth Street.

Not long after they moved out, the Thomas family moved in (pronounced Toe-Moss). They were a nice Mexican Catholic family.

"There are only two truly infinite things: the universe and foolishness. And I'm not so certain about the universe."

—Albert Einstein

The Prettiest Girl in Douglas

"Mom," I asked one day. "How did you and June ever meet?"

"Well, Daddy came home from work one day and said, 'I met the most beautiful woman coming through the port today. She's interested in attending our church. Why don't you call on her?' So the next day Mrs. Ingman and I called on her and invited her to church."

The Richardsons were transferred from El Paso to Douglas by the Southern Pacific Railroad. June—Mrs. Richardson—was a homemaker. Their two children, Tom and Margaret, were three and one year older than I. We were playmates and intimate friends until we all left Douglas. They lived on Twelfth Street across from the front door of Intermediate School. They had a TV, too.

It didn't take long for June and my mom to become fast friends. June regularly braided Mom's ultra-long hair and piled it atop her head. That was done at June's kitchen table and took three or four cups of coffee to get it all done. Mom always went over to June's house and we kids tagged along.

Over the years we grew into a close family. Dad and Earl had railroad interests. Tom and Margaret were the nearest thing that Ruth and I had to cousins. June and Mom were kitchen friends and close church ladies. They spent hours on the phone together. We became so close that we walked into each other's homes without knocking. Except me. I was uncomfortable about that and always politely knocked. They yelled through the door, "Come in!" And every time I went in, June said, "You don't have to knock at our house, honey."

Tom didn't come to our neighborhood very often. He had his own buddies. But when he did come over, he liked to read comic books up in my tree house and gobble our apricots. He enjoyed extracting honey with us, and sometimes worked hard right alongside us. For a couple of high school years he had his own hives of bees and Dad proudly helped him.

Their front yard was nice and wide. It made for a good football field. They had two big shady trees out near the curb which made for nice front yard fun. Once we sat on their front porch glider during a dangerous downpour and watched the wind whip those branches around.

Right after my 8th Grade year started my parents told me I'd be staying at June's house for a week or so.

"How come?"

"We're going on vacation to Kansas and taking Ruth with us. But you need to stay here and keep your school work going."

Two weeks without a little sister? Two weeks over at Tom's house? That sounded like a vacation I'd enjoy.

At the first evening meal I was served a few slices of fresh, home-grown tomatoes. *Oooh, yum-yum!* I remembered my manners and politely said, "Please pass the sugar."

Everyone looked at my plate. "What do you want sugar for?"

"My tomato slices."

"You don't put sugar on tomatoes! You put salt on tomatoes!"

"We do," I replied calmly.

"Well, you don't in this house. Here, use salt."

I had never put a granule of salt on my tomatoes, only sugar. "No, thank you," I replied politely.

"Well, I'm not passing you the sugar."

"Okay, do you have any honey? My dad puts honey on his tomatoes. It's good, too."

"No, Paul. But you may put salt on them."

I ate them plain, and the next night the sugar bowl was nowhere in sight.

Two weeks later, when my folks got back, the first thing said to them was, "He wanted to put sugar on his tomatoes! Where'd he learn that? And honey, too! Do you do that at your house?"

One evening during that stay, I went racing into the house, beelining for the bathroom. I shoved myself through the door and there was Margaret, standing over the sink, wearing nothing but her undies and a foamy toothbrush.

"*Aauughuugh!*" she gargled. I never opened and closed a door so fast in all my life.

Because Margaret was my near-sister/near-cousin since age three, she assumed an older sister role toward me. That was okay. I don't recall huffing and puffing at the sight of her like a normal, healthy 8th Grader. But I sure was embarrassed.

A few minutes later Margaret came out in a full robe. "At our house, when the bathroom door is closed, that means someone is in there. You should knock," she barked.

"Sorry," I said.

"Do like I do," Tom said with a big grin. "Go out in the alley behind the garage. It's dark; nobody will see you."

Later that evening as I gazed at their family photo on the mantle, I realized just how pretty June and Margaret were.

June was a tall, gracious beauty, even if she was a grownup. A stunner, indeed. Dad was right when he said "I met the most beautiful woman…" Margaret was a short beauty. A stunner, too, who eventually became one of our high school cheerleaders. Her smile can drain a watermelon. I was proud that she was our "sister." I was glad that Mom called on June long, long ago. For the record, Tom was a handsome young man, too. For the record again, I loved June and Earl, Tom and Margaret.

I was upset when they were transferred back to El Paso during my sophomore year in high school. I mean, they're family.

Some years later, a friend and I were discussing former classmates and agreed that Margaret Richardson was the prettiest girl who ever set foot in Douglas. And then he added, "Your sister Ruth was hot, too."

"…she was an intelligent and beautiful woman…"

—1 Samuel 25:3

Neal's Wedding

I was twelve when Neal married Beverly Watkins up in Tempe. They were students at Arizona State College; now ASU. Mom and Ruth took off a couple of days beforehand to help do something. On the big day, Dad and I rode the Greyhound bus.

And guess what! Before we even got on the bus, Dad asked me if I'd like a donut! Yeah! We sat in the first seat, right-hand side, where Dad talked with the driver. Then in Bisbee everybody got off the bus and went inside for a treat. I got another donut. Dad said it was okay. Then we stopped in Tombstone. I got a cinnamon roll with maple icing slathered all over it. First one of those I ever had. The best one, too. Just down the road, St. David was good for my first 7-Up of the day.

There was a nice long stop at the Horseshoe Café and Greyhound Bus Terminal in Benson. Syrupy pancakes and another 7-Up. In downtown Tucson, it was time for lunch. A fat hamburger and a Pepsi, and some jelly beans to take along. After that, we stopped up at Picacho Peak, out in the middle of the desert, so that required a refreshing sweet lemonade. Dad and I both got a tall bag of popcorn and the biggest *3 Musketeers* I ever saw.

•   •   •

Beautiful Downtown Benson Department: The Horseshoe Café is still there (2009).

•   •   •

In Casa Grande, Cracker Jacks. The prize inside was a little plastic hunting knife. And another Pepsi, too. What a day! What got into Dad?

It was payday for the Indians who lived on the Gila River reservation. They rode the bus to Phoenix. A few at a time stood beside Highway 80 out there in the middle of the hot desert and the bus stopped for them. They paid when they got on.

How many stops did we make for them? I don't know. Lots. There was standing room only by the time we got to Chandler.

There was room for a cool Barq's Orange soda. A funny discomfort began gnawing at my stomach about that time. I wonder what was wrong with that Orange soda?

Mesa, Arizona. I wasn't that hungry, but boy, did my stomach hurt. I complained to Dad. "Well, we'll be in Tempe next stop. You can lay down when we get there."

Next stop? Hah! What did he know? That pokey bus stopped all along Apache Boulevard—letting people slowly get off. It was more like a city bus. And then there were those ill-placed red lights. The bus stopped for every one of them, too. And my stomach—*good grief!*—it hurt!

I didn't feel like seeing. The sight of our wadded up popcorn bags curled my lips. The bus driver was noisily smacking on his own box of Cracker Jacks. "Oooh!" Somebody behind us was slurping through a straw. "*Sssloouuurrrrphpp!*" I didn't feel like hearing.

"There's that real good fried chicken place," Dad pointed out to the driver.

"Oh, yeah," the driver replied. "Colonel Sanders Kentucky Fried Chicken restaurant. You know what? They got sawdust all over the floor in there. But it's a good place to eat, alright. Serve real good iced tea, too. Already has sugar in it."

I didn't know whether to hold my stomach or hold my ears.

Late in the afternoon, we finally debarked in Tempe. Clutching my stomach with both hands, I moaned in the back seat of a car. I let my tears and sobs flows. The grown-ups were chattering all at once as they do when friends get together.

"Ooh. *Ooh!*" I told them.

"I'm afraid he doesn't want to lose Neal," Mom ignored, and kept on chattering away.

"Ooh. *Ooh!*" I repeated.

I never experienced pain like this before. What's wrong? At supper time, I declined (probably a first for me). "Now honey, we've got a long evening ahead of us. You need to eat something."

"Nuunngh!"

Neal and Beverly's wedding was longer than Queen Elizabeth's. I get a stomachache just thinking about it. I slumped next to Mom. I didn't cry out loud because I was such a polite little boy. But I sniffled as loud as possible. Strangers smiled at me sympathetically. "He must really love his big brother," they whispered.

The reception was longer! They got nine hundred gifts—more than that, but I lost count—and tenderly opened each one, slowly and carefully reading the cards that came with them. "Oh, this is just what we *need*. Look, Neal. Now we'll have a toaster for every room."

There was wedding cake and punch. *"Nuunngh!"*

It was my responsibility to deliver little plates of cake to people. I staggered around and somehow got it done, thick teardrops rolling down my cheeks. Those thick globs of sweet icing made me dizzy.

"Poor kid," the strangers said. "He must be upset that Neal's getting married."

"Isn't that sweet? I think he's been crying ever since he got here."

We rode the train home late that night. I dove onto a seat, curled up and farted so hard I was asleep within fifteen seconds.

I woke up the next morning feeling all better. Everybody still thinks I was bawling because my big brother got married. But really, there was an unusual pain in my stomach. I figure Neal and Beverly still owe me a piece of wedding cake.

Neal and Beverly's wedding is the only one of us kids' that my folks attended. The rest of us were married further across the country and more or less on a moment's notice.

• • •

Advice to Kids Department: Kids, no matter how much they insist, don't let your parents buy you anything you want.

• • •

"It is not good to eat too much honey…"

—Proverbs 25:27

Trips Out of Douglas

Except for a trip to California when I was three and the trips my folks took to Kansas when I was 13, we didn't take travel vacations. However, there were plenty of Southern Arizona car trips. Dad and I took the Greyhound bus up to Phoenix for Neal and Beverly's wedding. Ruth and Mom had already ventured up there. The whole family returned to Douglas on Southern Pacific's "Sunset Limited."

Local area trips included jaunts to Bisbee, Naco, Benson and Willcox. We went to Ft. Huachuca and Fry a couple of times. Went to Tombstone for a church function once. In the winter Dad kept several beehives in an Elfrida lettuce field, so we visited them a lot.

• • •

Changing Times Department: You won't find Fry, Arizona, on a map anymore. It's Sierra Vista now.

• • •

A few times I rode the school bus to a sport or music event in those same little towns. Many of those school trips went all the way to Tucson. Dad made trips to Tucson and Phoenix in a government car for government business. Our favorite trips were to Rucker Canyon or the Wonderland of Rocks, due north of Douglas. They are beautiful, cool, rocky, desert retreats. No wonder the Apaches enjoyed living there. We took out-of-town visitors there. They and I stood in awe of the balanced rocks the size of houses. When we had out-of-town company our family treated them (and ourselves) to all-day picnics and the cool air. It was in the Wonderland of Rocks where I picked my own *biyotes*, bitter little habit-forming nuts. I filled my pockets and ate them for two days. I'd like some now!

We didn't stray too far from home because my parent's cars were not that road-worthy. We had a two-door '37 Studebaker, (the one with the crunched fender). About 1953, Dad landed a real nice "new" '36 Chevy. I figured out how to drive in that car by carjacking it out of the yard. No one was home that Saturday and I was about the only one in the neighborhood not at the movies. I climbed in the car, started it up and drove up the street onto—yes, onto—the Clawson School grounds. I had so much adrenalin running through me that, without knowing what I was doing, I spun a really pretty donut, dust a-flying everywhere. I hurried back home, parked the car and hid in my tree house for half an hour. I wanted to be sure no police were cruising around looking for me. Apparently no one saw me, or if they did, didn't call the police—or my parents.

Dad was always conscientious about travel plans. Regardless of the distance or time we'd be gone, he always took spare radiator hoses, spare belts, plenty of extra water, a tire repair kit, a couple of quarts of oil and his tool box. On the trips I remember, he never used any of those things.

Many people drove across the desert with canvas water bags hanging from the hood ornament. We did that, too, with a couple of extra bags in the trunk to boot. It was not uncommon to see a car parked on the shoulder of the road, hood up, the driver patiently waiting for the radiator to cool down enough to open it and add more water.

Sooner or later, another driver pulled along side. "Need some help?"

"Naw, just gotta wait till she cools down some."

"Got plenty of water?"

"Yep."

Rich people had "air conditioning" in their cars. They bought little water coolers that were held in place by the rolled-up back seat window. They looked like miniature jet engines, bullet-shaped. As the car whizzed along the highway, hot desert air passed through the water and entered the car, cooling off everybody inside. That's what they told me anyway.

Our church sent kids to camp up on Mt. Lemmon near Tucson. As much as Dad wanted to drive a carload of kids up there, he had to let someone else take them, because he didn't trust our car to get us up the mountain. Later on, we went to camp in Prescott Pines in northern Arizona. That was definitely too far for Dad.

Those trips to Prescott were always fun. Here's the itinerary. Stop in Benson at the Horseshoe Café for a snack. Stop at Bob's Big Boy in Tucson for lunch. Stop in Phoenix for an afternoon snack at Sambo's Pancake House. Arrive at "Prescott Pines Baptist Campground" just in time for a big dinner. We repeated the stops on the way home.

When I was a high school sophomore four of us choir students went to Tempe to sing in the All-State Choir festival. Mr. Wildung, our choir director, drove. On the way back, he suggested a pizza pie for lunch. All of us were quiet. I was hungry. I wanted a big fat hamburger. Whoever heard of eating "a piece of pie" for lunch? Eventually someone quietly suggested, "Let's try something new." I went along with them. Mr. Wildung knew right where to go. When we arrived in Tombstone, he went directly to Allen Street and pulled up in front of a sit-down pizza pie restaurant. He ordered for everyone.

The waitress brought us empty plates. A few minutes later she set a big old round thing in the center of the table. It was piping hot and smelled pretty good. It was loaded with everything they had in the refrigerator. But we had to serve ourselves. I thought restaurants brought you a plate of food, didn't they?

Mr. Wildung reached into the pie and showed us how to help ourselves. I figured it couldn't be all bad if they let you help yourself with your hands. It couldn't be all bad if you didn't have to say, "Please pass the pizza." I politely waited for the girls to take their pieces. Then I stretched across my plate, pulled back a small experimental piece and took my first tentative bite of pizza pie. I've been gobbling them ever since.

Pastor Morgan took me and his daughter Carol to California one long weekend to check out BIOLA, a Christian college in downtown LA. I don't remember much about that trip except that the preacher busted me for sneaking a smoke. But he let me drive from Yuma to Tucson through the middle of the night. After breakfast in Tucson, I slept in the back of his station wagon all the way to our front door. My feet hung out the back end the whole way home.

• • •

Years Earlier Department. We visited Grandmother in Watsonville, California, when I was three. Somewhere there's a picture of me standing out on the beach, bundled up for the middle of winter. Along the way Dad had to change a tire beside the road. Mom and I sat on the bank of an irrigation ditch while Neal and Noel got to run all over the place. I wanted to run around, too, but Mom wouldn't let me. Ruth wasn't there, but there's a strong possibility she was conceived about then.

Two things I remember about Grandmother's house: we stepped down to enter her living room. And her front porch floor was painted dark green. Or did we step *up* to enter her living room? Or was it the walls that were dark green?

• • •

"... 'Go in peace. Your journey has the Lord's approval.' "

—Judges 18:6

Yes! Virginia!

Whenever I went to Prescott Pines for summer church camp, I really had only one thing on my mind: pretty girls. I wasn't the only one, either. And all the girls were guilty of the same thing—in reverse.

Mind you, the purpose of church camp is for spiritual revival, regardless of your age. But I didn't need camp for that. Why, I knew all the important Bible verses by heart. I had memorized the books of the Bible; knew exactly where they all were. I didn't need a hymn book to sing, because the words were chiseled into my mind. I knew the preacher's next sentence almost every time. For me, altar call was an exercise in patience, because I'd been there and done that ten times to the tenth power.

I was in junior high school the summer I met a pretty, tall, dark-haired, dark-complexioned girl from Tucson. Virginia Something. She was at Prescott Pines for the first time. In fact, this was her first "Sunday School" camp, as she called it.

"Hmmm," I thought, "here's a sweet, Christian girl." It looked like the potential for romance was boundless, so I quickly staked my claim to her. Early in the mornings we waited for each other for breakfast, then as time and activities allowed we were "together."

One evening after chapel service she let me walk her back to her cabin; that is, to the line that no boy could cross, affectionately referred to as "No Man's Land." Virginia and I had several minutes before curfew, so naturally we took a long, round-about trail. We paused to sit on some wooden steps and chat.

A recent rain had cleaned the air and the wet, northern Arizona pine smelled deliciously fresh. Enough clouds had moved away that the moon shone gently upon us. We were in the perfect setting for me to steal a kiss, which was my original intent from the get-go. Convinced that I'd receive one freely offered, I snuggled up close and held her hand.

But there was a tear in her eye. Uh-oh, what's this?

I don't know what came over me, but I just blurted out: "Virginia, are you sure that the Lord is in your heart?"

She lowered her head. Her long dark hair hid her face from me. She was crying and sniffling now. Gently and honestly she shook her head.

Astonished, I had no idea what to do next. She looked like she was saved. I mentally fumbled for words. What do I say? Quote scripture? Preach? Point my finger at all her sins? She sure looked like a sweet Christian girl to me.

I, Paul Nichols, in church every Sunday, student of the Bible, altar call veteran, son of a Baptist deacon, and a fourteen-year-old religious expert didn't know what to do or say. But I was just close enough to my spiritual roots to know that this moment better not pass without offering Virginia a way to know that Jesus was in her heart.

I let go of her hand. "Do you want to pray?' I asked.

She nodded and whispered, "But I don't know what to say." A tear dropped onto the step between her shoes.

Speechless, almost thoughtless, I took a deep breath and said, "Well, uh…I'll pray and you, uh…just repeat, okay?"

"Alright."

Pray what? It took me awhile to get started, what with my throat being so dry and my heart pounding so hard. I guess when you're at your wit's end you just have to move over for the Lord. Only Jesus knows what I prayed or what Virginia repeated, but when we said "Amen," Virginia was a brand new Christian.

The Lord is ever merciful. And He's creative about it, too. About that time, we spied an adult counselor walking across the grounds. We caught up with him. He wanted to know why we were out past curfew. We told him of Virginia's prayer. I was relieved that he took over.

The Lord is also a pretty good parent, if you think about it. My own cabin counselor happened along looking for me. He saw us and insisted that I return to my cabin right then.

After camp, Virginia and I wrote each other a few letters and I saw her about six months later in a Tucson church. I haven't seen her since. I'll see her again in heaven, though. I'll say, "You're the first person I ever prayed with."

She'll say, "Really? Praise the Lord." Then we'll praise the Lord some more.

And I'll interrupt and ask, "And what's your last name again?"

•   •   •

P.S. Department: I never did steal that kiss.

•   •   •

"If you confess with your mouth, 'Jesus is Lord,' and believe in your heart that God raised him from the dead, you will be saved."

—Romans 10:9

Debbie, Cozette and Valerie—and Jeannine

One pleasant September day when Noel and his wife Lavonda were home on Army leave, he sat at our kitchen table as cool as his cucumber lunch.

"Hi," I said when I came home for lunch. "Did you have the baby?"

"Yeah."

I was an uncle again.

"Boy or girl," I asked.

"A little girl," he said, unruffled.

"What's her name?"

"Cozette Aileen," he said proudly.

Cozette was Noel and Lavonda's second daughter. She was the tiniest, too, weighing in around four pounds, so she had to stay in an incubator a little while. Debbie was born in Germany. Cozette is a Douglas native. Valerie was born in Georgia a couple of years after Cozette.

Trivia: Dr. Duncan delivered four of my parent's children and one of their grandchildren.

By the time Cozette was born, my folks had purchased Mr. and Mrs. Mason's house next door. What a great, rent-free place for Lavonda and the girls to stay while Noel spent some Army time in Korea.

Dad cut a gate in the fence between our yards for easy access to either. The girls were over in our house a lot. I helped them in and out of my tree house. And we were in their house quite a bit, too.

One winter night I dashed over to Lavonda's screaming, *"It's a boy! It's a boy!"* The next night I reran the whole scenario, only I yelled, *"It's a girl! It's a girl!"*

Here's why. Neal and Beverly called long distance to announce that they were about to adopt a baby boy. Well, the next day they discovered they'd been given the wrong information. So they adopted Jeannine, my cute little niece.

Lavonda had a little TV, so Ruth and I and a friend or two squeezed into her little living room to watch old movies. It helped relieve a little of her loneliness. She only got Channel 9 out of Tucson. It played old movies, commercials, some news—that's about it.

Debbie, Cozette and Valerie cuddled themselves up to me during those TV movies. I encouraged them and sometimes ended up with all three of them in my lap. I got along so well with them that I got to babysit a few times. I learned to change diapers on Cozette and Valerie. No, not Pampers—cotton diapers, which had to be folded a certain way and then pinned just so to keep them on tight. Oh, and those diapers had to be rinsed out in the toilet and washed and hung out on the line to dry. Day after day.

I was such a natural with those girls that Lavonda and my parents let me wash several loads of diapers and hang them on the clothes line. Am I good or what? Why, I'm so good they even let me take them in and fold them up, too. I put them in a "diaper stacker" that hung on the end of a crib.

Here's an easy way to make Lavonda mad. One Saturday Dad ran some errands downtown and took Cozette along with him. She happened to be wearing a pair of coveralls—like Granddaddy's. Now, Cozette's brilliant white hair was cut short, like a cute little Dutch Boy cut. But it was kind of stringy and unkempt, hanging into her eyes, so Dad stopped into a barber shop and asked the barber to "...trim it up a little."

The barber went right to work. "Buzz, buzz" went his buzzer.

It didn't take too many strokes for Dad to interrupt. "That's a little close for her, isn't it?"

"Her? Isn't this a little boy?"

"No! This is my grand*daughter*!" Dad said.

Oops.

"Oh, uh, well, in these coveralls... Okay, no problem. I can fix this up real cute."

Snip, snip went his scissors—very carefully.

Nope, it was too late. Fixing it up real cute was out of the question. But it was a problem. Cozette looked like a little Dutch boy with hair high on the sides, and a regular little boy with hair high on the back. Her bangs got severely shortened.

Back at the house, Mom didn't know whether to laugh or to cry. Remember, several years earlier I did the same thing to my sister—*for free!* Lavonda was so upset that her own hair almost spontaneously combusted. Dad wasn't allowed within fifty yards of Cozette till Noel got home a year later.

That's how easy it is to make Lavonda mad.

But here's an easy way to make Lavonda happy. Lavonda and Noel were high school sweethearts and maintained a wholesome and admirable courtship. From what little I knew of love, I guessed that both of them were destined for marriage and a baby carriage. But alas, Lavonda's family moved to Arkansas during Noel's senior year.

Noel joined the Army immediately after he graduated. About a year later he found himself in Ft. Campbell, Kentucky. Wouldn't you know it? That's not too far from the little town where Lavonda's family had moved. First chance he got, he made a trip to the little town. And wouldn't you know it again? As he walked along Main Street, he spied Lavonda walking along, too.

"Hey, Lavonda," he called.

She thought she was dreaming of his familiar voice, but turned around anyway. Noel proposed within hours and married her within days.

That's how easy it is to make Lavonda happy.

> *"For great is your love, reaching to the heavens;*
> *your faithfulness reaches to the skies."*

—Psalm 57:10 and Psalm 108:4

Burma Shave Signs

"I see a Burma-Shave sign up ahead," Dad said as he drove along the highway. We kids in the back leaned up over the front seat, peering hard through the windshield.

"I see 'em!" one of us always yelled.

In a minute Mom always exclaimed, "Here it is!"

A '50s trip was no trip at all without Burma Shave signs. They helped break up the monotony of a hot trip to somewhere. If you were sleeping, we woke you up so you wouldn't miss the Burma-Shave sign. They were all along American highways. Little red boards on a stick. White lettering. Five or six of them. Lined up 1/4 mile apart. Advertising shaving cream. They were short, pithy poems. They always ended "...Burma Shave." Beloved Americana. In the end, there were about 7,000 of 'em delighting our roadsides. They stood from 1930 to 1963.

Here's some samples:

> Are your whiskers...
> > [*Drive 1/4 of a mile*]
> When you wake...
> > [*Drive 1/4 of a mile*]
> Tougher than...
> > [*Drive 1/4 of a mile*]
> A two bit steak?
> > [*Drive 1/4 of a mile*]
> *Burma Shave*

Always a favorite of mine (near Lordsburg, NM?).

> My cheek...
> Said she...
> Is smooth as satin...
> Ha Ha Said he...
> That's mine you're pattin'.
> *Burma Shave*

The Burma Shave sign between Douglas and Bisbee said,

> She kissed the hairbrush…
> By mistake…
> She thought it was…
> Her husband, Jake.
> *Burma Shave*

We got excited every time we saw it and read it aloud, sometimes in unison, every time we passed it.

Burma Shave signs were…well, Burma Shave signs.

> *"Gone the signs, gone the lines…*
>
> *Wry and sassy, even classy…*
>
> *We loved them…*
>
> *Lines of signs by…*
>
> *Burma Shave"*

> —Paul Nichols, but please don't tell anybody

161

Deep in the Heart of Kansas

I was sixteen and I had a driver's license. Mom and Dad surprised me one evening when they said, "Well, how would you like to spend the summer with Pat and Lloyd?" They are my married cousins who lived in Quinter, Kansas, on an 800-acre wheat farm. The day after school was out, Dad stuck Ruth and me in the '53 Buick and off we went for Kansas. Mom stayed home.

The first night we stopped in Tucumcari, New Mexico, to stay with my parent's friends. They were old and thin vegetarians who served us something grayish I never heard of and didn't recognize. I only ate it because I was such a polite—er, hungry—young man. The next morning I opted for oatmeal for breakfast because it was the only gray thing I recognized. Just before we drove off, Dad left a half gallon of honey with them. About an hour down the road, Dad said, "Pull in there," pointing to a white and red roadside restaurant. We wolfed down bacon and bacon and bacon.

We made it to Quinter that evening and were welcomed with a feast of fried chicken, beef, corn on the cob, vegetables, piles of biscuits and cornbread, and four or five cakes and pies. Pat can cook!

Next day, Lloyd gave us a little tour of his wheat farm, which was passed down to him from his father and grandfather. There are covered wagon ruts running through one of his cow pastures. Deep tracks running across virgin land—untouched, except by bison, Indians and cows. American land that lay just the way it was when the Lord finished creating it. It's an impressive historical feature, and Lloyd was justifiably proud of it.

Dad and Ruth left a case of honey behind, then took off for Douglas. I was left to stare at skies with no mountains. How does the sun rise? I was lonely for mountains already. How does the moon come up? I shivered in the bright sunshine, almost wishing I was riding horses with Doug Foster.

"We got mountains," Lloyd assured me. "They're just half a day from here over in Colorado."

To cure any homesickness, Lloyd taught me right away how to drive a little Case tractor and pull a one-way plow. He plowed a few rows while I sat on the fender. "Will it hurt anything if I run over some rocks?" I asked him.

"You won't hit any rocks," he assured me. Huh? What? Impossible. It was dirt, wasn't it? But he was right. There's not a single rock in western Kansas. Just plain dirt. I also noticed that after dark the stars seemed a little further away.

Pat and Lloyd's two children, Judy and Jarrell, were several years younger than I, but I played with them a little every day. Otherwise, I spent the whole summer working and eating. I plowed several fields, fed chickens and cows, ran errands into town and did whatever Lloyd asked of me. He paid me a dollar a day, fed me all I wanted and let me sleep in the house.

Their house was a tornado shelter, a complete house with a flat roof about three feet above ground. Tiny windows circled the house to let in daylight. It was as normal as any other house, just underground. It always smelled like fried chicken and fresh baked biscuits. I'm telling you, Pat knows how to cook!

It was really an uneventful summer until the two weeks of wheat harvest—the last two weeks of June. Lloyd got me up well before daylight for a hearty breakfast. Into the wheat fields we went with headlights shining. Lloyd drove the combine and I drove the truck. When the truck was full, I drove it to the grain elevator in beautiful downtown Quinter, where it was weighed, emptied and weighed again. I went back for another load.

The best part of wheat harvest was seeing Patsy come out into the field about nine o'clock with another breakfast. She came out at lunch time with sandwiches and fried chicken and pie and lots of iced tea. About four o'clock she came with some more of the same, and had a nice hot dinner on the table when we came in after dark.

I was excused from harvest on Sunday to go to church with Pat and the little kids. Lloyd was nervous about possible rain, so he stayed back and kept on combining. We got it all harvested in just over a week. "When I get rich, I'm thinking about having one of those combine crews come in and combine for me. Won't take them but one day to do my fields," Lloyd said wistfully.

We celebrated 4tha July with little fireworks over a field that just last week was full of amber waves of grain.

Then we took a trip to "our mountains" in Colorado. Their friends, the Lehman family, went along, too. They rented a couple of cabins on a beautiful high-mountain lake. I was so excited to see rocks that within ten minutes I was skipping them across the lake. I threw rocks just for the sake of throwing them. Everybody giggled at me, but I was so happy to be on a mountain full of rocks that I didn't care. They were pretty mountains, too, with Christmas trees all over them.

Next day, I caught my first rainbow trout. Then I caught my limit and ate them that night. Delicious! Same thing every day for a week. We visited the Royal Gorge before (sadly) returning to Quinter.

**My first trout — from a Colorado mountain lake. It was delicious.
Summer 1959.**

Just a few days later, my family and Mom's sister, Aunt Crosie, showed up—with more honey. In a day or two we headed for Memphis, Tennessee, and Columbus, Georgia. Dad let me drive a lot.

Somewhere on a lonely Oklahoma highway Ruth had to go to the bathroom. We pulled into a wobbly roadside gas station—the kind you see in those nostalgic paintings—and Dad asked the young man for $1.50 of regular. He then offered to pay with a two dollar bill.

"I cain't take this, suh," the kid said.

"How come?" Dad asked.

"That ain't real," the kid chuckled.

"Sure it is," Dad said.

"I ain't never seen one of them before. It's pretty neat, but I cain't take it."

"Why, this is just as good as any other money," Dad assured him.

"No, suh. You need to pay with something else."

Dad paid with something else. Back on the lonely highway Aunt Crosie suggested, "He probably thinks you were trying to get five gallons of free gas and steal fifty cents, too."

In Memphis, we stayed with old Aunt Lillian, a frumpy, world-class bigot and racist. She introduced me and Ruth to words and terms we never knew existed. While Dad drove, she led us on a tour of Memphis cemeteries, pointing out the graves of our ancient relatives. She maintained an earthy, fast-paced, detailed commentary of all their funerals. At a gas station she snapped at me for almost going into a restroom that didn't have a "Whites Only" sign on it. I'm not sure which was more unnerving: her crass remark, the sign, or the filthy white restroom. Back at her house she proudly showed us the blue dress she planned to wear to her own funeral. Dad left her a small jar of honey, and we hurried off for Columbus, Georgia.

We visited Noel and Lavonda and his houseful of pretty girls in Columbus, Georgia. He and Lavonda got a whole case of honey. After two days, we found US Highway 80 and headed for Douglas.

It was a good summer. I enjoyed working and eating on the farm. The week in the Colorado mountains was good medicine. Dad let me drive across America the Beautiful more than he did. Little did I know that just four years later I'd return to Columbus and marry a pretty girl of my own.

"...Put some of the best products of the land in your bags and take them down to the man as a gift—a little balm and a little honey..."

—Genesis 43:11

The Tall Part of Dad

Dad loved tall tales. His friend Mr. Evans did, too. Mr. Evans' favorite was the story of the time he met a ferocious bear in the woods. The bear rose up on its hind legs and opened its mouth to gobble up Mr. Evans. But Mr. Evans stuck his hand down the bear's throat, reached way down, grabbed the bear's tail and yanked real hard. Well, that turned the bear inside-out and it ran off in the opposite direction.

He told that story time and again. My dad always replied, "Well, now, that ain't the way I heard it," and regaled us with something like...

- Some folks don't like our Arizona weather. I don't know why. Why, the air in Arizona is so nice, those folks in Los Angeles will drive to Yuma just to fill their tires with it.

- Course, Arizona does get rather hot. Where else do hens lay hard boiled eggs?

- I myself have seen rain, but I sure do wish my boys could see it rain once.

- It's so dry here, we have to take our frogs to the city pool and give 'em swimmin' lessons.

- But things are worse in Oklahoma where I grew up. Terribly finicky weather there. There was one Spring afternoon it was so hot, a farmer died of sunstroke while he was out plowing. Well, naturally he was late for supper, so his wife went out looking for him. By the time she found him it was after dark and by then he had froze solid.

- Ya' know, in Oklahoma, it gets so cold that there's two inches between the degree marks on the thermometer.

166

Mr. Evans returned, "That reminds me: up in Nebraska it got so cold one winter that when we talked we had to carry our words inside and thaw 'em out to hear what we said."

And Dad said, "Well, that ain't the way I heard it. I heard Nebraska got so hot that summer, that the popcorn popped right off the stalks."

"Oh, it was mighty hot, yes sir," said Mr. Evans.

"Trouble was," Dad continued, "The cows saw all that popcorn coming down and thought it was snow. So they just stood there and froze to death."

"I had some cows once," Mr. Evans recalled. "Little cows. Smallest cows you ever seen. Every spring, the new little calves got littler than the year before. Pretty soon, they was littler than a peanut. So little that I branded 'em with my wife's hat pin. I finally had to give up on 'em. Yep, they got so little that it took 'em a week just to walk across a map of Nebraska."

Dad and I were on Ninth Street, only a few steps from the Owl Drug Store one warm Saturday afternoon. "Want to get some ice cream?" he casually asked.

"Yeah!" I said.

He knew I had a pocketful of pocket change, so he said, "Well, why don't you loan me a dollar and we'll get some."

"Uh, okay," I said, reaching for my coins.

"Well, wait a minute," he said. "Only give me fifty cents of it. That way, I'll owe you fifty cents as soon as we get home. But you'll still owe me fifty cents. So just keep it and we'll be even."

"???"

"God has brought me laughter, and everyone who hears about this will laugh with me."

—Genesis 21:6

The Dimmer Part of Dad

Dad never let on when he pulled one over on you. And few people ever pulled one over on him.

He had two strong opinions. "Only good thing ever come outta Texas is Highway 80."

And. "Automatic transmissions! Huh! If you're too lazy to shift gears, then you oughta just get yourself a horse!" he ranted every chance he got. "They couldn't have thought up a worse thing to do to cars." Therefore, he only purchased vehicles with manual transmissions. My poor, short mom.

At the end of my Kansas summer, Aunt Crosie joined us there to continue on to Noel's house in Georgia. Now, Pat and Lloyd took me to Aunt Crosie's house in Manhattan two times that summer (She is Pat's mom). I noticed she had a car with an automatic transmission. Not only that, but she had an automatic light-dimming switch mounted on the dashboard.

Normally, to dim the headlights for oncoming cars, drivers used the left foot to press a floor button. "*Chunka*." To ask approaching drivers to dim their lights, we pressed it twice. "*Chunka-Chunka*." To get the bright lights shining again, we pressed the button again. Not Aunt Crosie. Her automatic switch did all the work for her at just the right time.

After we left Georgia, Dad and I sat in the front most of the time. Ruth, Mom and Aunt Crosie sat in the back, chattering across the country. I was driving west somewhere in East Texas on Highway 80. Everyone was awake and alert, admiring the tall pines and the busy oil wells.

I quietly remarked about automatic transmissions, my first ever opportunity to pull one over on Dad.

Just as I figured, Dad jumped on that. "No, siree! That's just pure laziness! If you're too lazy to shift gears, then get yourself a horse!" he ranted. "And they cost more, too! Save yourself some money and get yourself a little exercise at the same time. It ain't going to kill you to move the gear shifter. Just pure-dee laziness!"

His pomposity was perfectly primed.

"Well, Dad," I said, so that Aunt Crosie heard me in the back seat, "what about those things that automatically dim your headlights?"

"Now *that's* laziness!" He pomped. "Why, whoever heard...who's so lazy they can't even press their foot down?" He got to rant about fifteen seconds.

"Now, just a minute, Nick!" Aunt Crosie shouted from the back seat. "I've got one of those in my car, and I don't know how I ever got along without it!" Suddenly Dad flinched and stared straight ahead. "It knows just when to dim," Aunt Crosie went on. "I don't have to worry about being too close. Nobody ever flashes their lights at me." She leaned up over the front seat. "And I'm not lazy, either, because I have to press the button anyway to get them back to brights!" Dad flinched again.

"I never...!" she said, throwing herself back into her seat. "Lazy! *Harrumph!*"

Dad put his pompous tail between his legs and never mentioned anything automatic again. I turned my head to admire all those East Texas oil wells along Highway 80, and to hide a big ornery grin.

I never let on that I pulled that one over on Dad.

• • •

Can You Believe This? Department: The last two cars Dad ever bought, used Buicks, had automatic transmissions.

• • •

"The first to present his case seems right, until another comes forward and questions him."

—Proverbs 18:17

169

Dances With Wolves and Sleeps With Snakes

He was always kind to me, always proud of me. I loved Buster. If you want to know what he looked like, take a good look at the actor Graham Greene. Mr. Greene starred in *Dances with Wolves* and *Maverick* (among others) and is occasionally featured on my favorite TV show, "The Red Green Show." Whenever I see Mr. Greene, I see Buster.

I never knew his last name. In fact, I never knew his given name at all. Buster was—and is—good enough for me. He was a stocky, solid, Mexican man, who spoke English without an accent and exercised a great, but corny, sense of humor. Buster lived alone out on sixty desert acres, not far from D Hill. It was easy to get to his lonely adobe house. We drove up a desert dirt road leading to a loose barbed wire gate. How many times did I drag that wobbly gate across the cattle guard to let Dad drive through, and then drag it back?

"Always leave a gate the way you found it," Dad told me a hundred times. Dad kept a few beehives out on Buster's property, which is why we went there a few times a month. Buster always seemed pleased to see us. Dad gave him honey, but I don't remember us giving him anything else like we did for people over across the line.

It was primarily at Buster's where I learned to shoot. Shotguns and .22s. The first time I ever fired a shotgun, the hammer scratched my face something terrible. And my shoulder hurt so much! A 10-gauge shotgun has a lot of kick for a young boy. But I wanted to do it again right away.

I had many good times shooting old cans and bottles. I was only allowed to shoot toward the north. Nothing but desert as far as the eye could see, with some low hills behind that. I sent a lot of glass in that direction. I liked to shoot at a certain large rock and listen to the ricochet go sirening across the desert.

Buster was an alcoholic. He walked to Agua Prieta to drink for a few days, then walked back home to drink some more. I'd say that was about seven miles, one way. Around his house were several three-foot piles of empty liquor bottles, each bottle tenderly placed there by him. There were plenty of beer cans, too. Several piles of them, and a lot just scattered around. Apparently he never threw the bottles out to let them break. And he shouldn't have. He always walked barefoot. But then again, who know? Maybe they might come in handy someday.

His outhouse was set up behind the tallest pile of bottles. A few chickens pecked around. He had a lazy hound that understood Spanish, but not English.

Buster had huge feet, well-calloused and unafraid of the hot desert ground. I specifically remember, about age six or so, being amazed at the size of his feet. Evidently, he had no socks, because even when he wore his great big, brown and dusty unlaced boots, he wore none.

From those piles of cans and bottles, I carried off a gunny sack load and set them up on a rusting car body. Blam, blam, blam! I shot, shot, shot. I set them up again and fired away some more.

Buster had a dozen old car bodies rusting away on his property. It was okay to shoot holes in them. And shoot holes in them we did. One day Noel and I blasted all the windows out of the most recent arrival.

A couple of times, I spied a cottontail rabbit, shot it and proudly gave it to Buster. His rattlesnakes got to have it for dinner. That was rare, though, because we made so much noise that the rabbits laid low till we left. Rabbits are too easy to shoot because if they hear a threatening noise they'll almost always freeze in place. Sometimes they're not much different than shooting bottles.

His rattlesnakes? Buster used a long pole with a loop on one end to capture snakes. He put them in three little wire cages, which he kept under his sleeping cot. He fed them rabbits to fatten them up. Pretty soon he ate them. (After a rattler swallows a rabbit, it bulges for two days until the rabbit is fully digested.) He gave me a bite one time and it was good. A Mason jar half full of rattles sat in Buster's window sill.

Buster's property had a clean area about the size of a football field. There were no whiskey bottles, no beer cans, no rusting cars, no piles of scrap metal—nothing, just low scrub brush and some weary yucca cactus. It was one of my favorite places. Dad let me drive his pickup around and around that field.

I was twelve years old. I knew how to drive a pickup, shift gears, speed up, slow down, brake correctly, you name it. At age twelve, I drove as well as any grown-up. And I owe it all to the practice field out at Buster's.

One day, Buster asked Dad, "Say, Mr. Nichols. Did your bees smell funny or anything when you were looking at them?"

"No, why?"

"Well, I had a little trouble with them this morning."

Dad was taken aback. The bees were a hundred yards away from the house. Trouble?

"I was cooking myself up some real good flapjacks and a pork chop. Just when I set 'em on the table, a swarm of bees came through the window and dropped nearly a half pint of honey all over my flapjacks."

I was eight or so years old. "I never heard of anything like that," I thought in astonishment. Dad's eyes lit up and a sly little grin developed. "Well, what was your trouble?"

"Trouble was, they took my pork chop back to the hive." He paused a moment, then added, "The honey was good, though."

Buster's house had two rooms plus a screened-in side porch that didn't amount to much. Unfinished liquor bottles were thick in there. His main room had a cast-iron wood stove, a little table and his sleeping cot. A kerosene lamp hung from the ceiling because he had no electricity. Loaded rifles stood in a corner. His other room, the front room, had boxes upon boxes of magazines. There was an old couch in there but it was covered with boxes upon boxes of magazines. His house may have looked like the city dump, but it was really quite a cozy place. Outside, too.

In the corner of the front room stood the prize of Cochise County. Few people knew of it; Buster, his sister and us. "I'm gonna give you that some day," he told me several times. Dad, ears waggling with covetousness, heard him every time. He promised me his tall Victrola phonograph, complete with two dozen round, blue cylinder recordings of violin music, and some of the great tenor, Enrico

Caruso. I considered it mine because Buster said so. Dad considered it his because I was his kid.

Buster showed me how to put the cylinders in place, then crank the Victrola, set the needle and listen. The scratchy, uneven sound came out of a big megaphone. It was an impressive bequeath. It was neat, and Buster let me play it several times.

One merciless hot midday out at Buster's when I was six or so, Dad was deep into his bees. He let me sit in the pickup—the only shady place in Cochise County that day. Buster wandered along and volunteered to take me back to his house and let me rest inside. It was so hot that he was wearing his unlaced boots. He carried me all the way back. He set me down and said, "It's a little cooler in here. Just lie down on my bed." I soon fell asleep on his cot.

Dad was fiery angry when he came back to the house for me. He got all over Buster for putting me down just six inches above three cages of rattlesnakes.

"Aw, I fed them good this morning. They just want to sleep themselves. They won't hurt nothing right now."

One morning Dad hammered on my shed door at six-thirty in the morning. He was supposed to be at work on the graveyard shift. I never knew Dad to leave work early.

"Paul, get up! Buster died last night!" I jumped out of bed and into my clothes in a flash. This was a special mission and I knew why. Off we hurried to Buster's. His gate was open; the only time I ever saw it so.

We dashed into Buster's house. Everything was in place including snakes and loaded rifles, but someone had already taken the Victrola. I'm telling you, that didn't set well with Dad.

"How did Buster die?" I asked on the way back home.

"Too much drinkin'." Buster died after he passed out in an Agua Prieta alley. He's the first person whose death made me sad. I missed him already and wondered about his soul. It took several months for Dad to convince Buster's sister that *we did not* take the Victrola. I think it made Dad feel better to know she didn't get it either. But who did?

About two years later, I drove out to Buster's "just to see." The barbed wire gate was replaced with a shiny, new steel gate that was padlocked shut. I stood by the gate and saw that his acres were swept clean. The old car bodies gone. His cozy adobe house bulldozed away. The desert had taken over. The snakes had to find their own rabbits.

I love Buster.

> "...and he had a leather belt around his waist.
> His food was locusts and wild honey."

—Matthew 3:4

Was Mrs. Ward Left-handed?

I knew Mrs. Ward from the time I was in third or fourth grade at Clawson School. She was not my teacher then, but her room was next to ours. I also saw her around church quite a bit. A member of Mom's Sunday School class, I figured she figured that any son of Mrs. Nichols was the next best thing to perfection—good-looking, too. From time to time, she made nice remarks to me, both at school and at church. It was quite apparent that she thought I was a nice young man.

Then came the 8th Grade and we got formally connected. I don't even remember what class Mrs. Ward taught. Anyway, my desk was in the row that faced the classroom door. The row was next to a wall of blackboards. My seat was the second or third one back. On a good day, it was easy to see into Mrs. Wein's English class across the hall.

One warm day, Paul McDonald and Lee Don Collier got into trouble with Mrs. Ward and she sent them out to the hall. When she wasn't looking, I plucked an eraser off the blackboard next to me and threw it at the boys out in the hall. *Hoo-haw!*

Oh, junk! They sent it back. It looked like a mouse gliding lazily along the floor. It came to rest just inches from my shoe. Mrs. Ward saw *that*! Her eyes were the size of moon pies. I stared transfixed in disbelief while Paul and Lee Don laughed in the hallway. Off she marched to confront Paul and Lee Don. I figured she'd be back, so I was trying to figure a way to flush myself through the floor as quickly as possible.

Within a splash of a moment, she spun on her wide heels, stomped back into the room and tromped right up to me, her eyes all ablaze. She took my chin in her right hand—brimstone spurting from her eyes—and slapped my face with her left hand. Paul and Lee Don and I traded places. "*...and stay there! I don't want to see you again!*" I had to stay inside a fire escape room. It was quiet throughout the known universe.

The next day, when it was time for her class, I went straight to that room. About ten minutes into the class time I overheard her say,

"Where's Paul Nichols?" Sharon Utke confessed that I was out there. Mrs. Ward came out and asked me if I was okay, and "What are you doing out here?"

"Well, you told me to stay out here."

"Not always."

I never told my parents what happened. She didn't either. It is my understanding that after class that warm day, Mrs. Ward wept.

"Those who sow in tears will reap with songs of joy."

—Psalm 126:5

It Was David Bond

I never liked math that much. Come on, come on, just accept what I say and don't try to convince me otherwise. I had a hard time with math. Today, I can balance my checkbook because I have a calculator.

But back in the eighth grade, Mrs. Phillips taught our math. Let me tell you something: Mrs. Phillips knew her math like my mother knew her English grammar. Mrs. Phillips was a small, thin woman who wore thick-rimmed glasses. She always smiled on the first and last days of school. Otherwise, she was a no-nonsense teacher and ruled her classroom and nearby hallway with an iron fist.

Lee Don Collier was big. Luis Rodriquez was big. Edmond Lewis was big. A few other guys were big. But Mrs. Phillips had "the look." "The look" trumped big eighth grade boys every time. It trumped little eighth grade boys like me every time, too. It trumped a whole classroom, including the girls.

Mrs. Phillips' classroom was on the second floor of the Junior High building and the windows were often open. Fortunately, no direct sunshine came in those windows, otherwise we might have spent most of our classes really snoring, instead of just sneaking a little doze.

And one day in math, when an unusually pleasant breezed wafted into the classroom, we were all having a grand time learning something about squares and rectangles and odd shaped things. Mrs. Phillips was in an unusually happy mood. She fired off question after question about the math stuff on the blackboard. "And what's this?" Somebody raised a hand and answered. "And this?" An answer. "And what about this?" Another answer. The kids fired back answer after answer. She had taught us well. Until she drew a square with a line from the SW corner to the NE corner. "And this?"

"The base of two triangles!"

"Aah, nope."

"Uh, An angular line."

"No."

"Obtuse?"

"Obtuse? "No!" (I think I detected a "look.")

"Straight?"

"No!"

We probably offered ten more guesses, but it was fruitless. None of us—not even those math whizzes Sharon Utke and Kathy Boyd— knew what Mrs. Phillips was looking for.

"This is ridiculous!" Mrs. Livid said. "Can't anyone tell me what kind of line this is? Look at it!" She stuck her pointer up against the slanted line she'd drawn and commanded, "Tell me what kind of line it is!" Then came "The Look." Sure enough. There it was. The room was deathly silent. No one moved.

Mrs. Phillips sat down at her desk with that "look" and said, "Alright, this is the last class of the day, so we'll just sit here till somebody tells me what kind of line I have drawn on the board. I don't have any plans for this evening, so if you want to stay here all night, it's fine with me. So think about it. This is as far as we're going till I hear the answer!" She sat down at her desk and opened her grade book.

Why is it that when everyone has to be really quiet, somebody always coughs?

"Who was that?" Mrs. Phillips snapped. Somebody raised a hand. "Do you know what kind of line that is?"

[*Cough.*] "No, ma'am." [*Cough, cough*]

"Then be quiet!" She "looked."

"Sorry," [*Cough.*"]

We weren't having a grand time anymore.

Finally, after ten minutes of shivering, shuddering silence, David Bond meekly raised his hand. Mrs. Phillips acknowledged him.

"Is it slanted?" he gently asked.

"What? Speak up. I can't hear you when you mumble."

"Slanted?" He spoke up.

"Yes!" she said. "Finally. It's a slanted line. Thank you, David. Doesn't anyone know something as simple as a slanted line?" She rose to pace the room and give us a heavy homework assignment. I never liked math homework.

While she paced, I looked at the back of David's head and decided that he must be a genius. He came up with such a simple answer.

Then suddenly, the expression "thinking outside the box" leapt into my mind. David Bond must have been thinking outside the box. He had to be. Most simple answers are outside the box, aren't they? David Bond was my hero for a few days.

I've tried to think outside the box ever since. One of the things I thought of is: let's outlaw math teachers.

$2^{32582657}-1$ *is the largest known Prime Number.*
It has 9,808,358 digits.

—I'll bet Mrs. Phillips doesn't know that.

Coach Sharp Had Only One Rule

I was in the seventh grade when Coach Sharp came to the Douglas school system. He was pumpkin-shaped and talked of a faraway place called Arkansas. He didn't have any kids then. He and his wife, Billie, lived on Mission Drive and attended their neighborhood Southern Baptist Church. While I was in school, Coach Sharp was the junior high PE teacher, assistant high school football coach, the high school baseball coach and taught Driver Education classes. As big as he was, he outran any kid in school. His name is Ike, spelled C-O-A-C-H.

It was apparent from his first day in Douglas that he was interested in every student that meandered through his classes. He was interested in them as students, as athletes and as honorable young men and women. He wanted only the best for each one of us, which is why he was unafraid to discipline us. Coach Sharp had only one rule: "No popping towels in the showers."

It wasn't long before Albert Pedrego and I reminded each other that rules were made to be broken. Naked, after a shower in the Junior High School gym, Albert and I exchanged a couple of good snaps. "*Snap!*" went my towel. "*Snap!*" went Albert's.

I heard Coach coming and made a beeline for my locker. Coach saw Albert take one last futile fling at me, but because a wall blocked his view, he didn't see me.

"Come here, Albert!" Coach bellowed.

Albert wrapped his towel around his waist and stood next to Coach's desk. Coach opened his lower desk drawer and withdrew a wicked wooden paddle. "Stand right here," he told Albert. "Drop that towel on the floor." No one had ever seen that paddle before and we all got real quiet. Nobody breathed.

That paddle had a personality. It was hungry and anxious. Eyeing that paddle, Albert reluctantly dropped his towel and started to shake. The paddle took one look at Albert's bare back side and waggled with anticipation. I dried and dressed faster than anyone in the history of locker rooms.

Coach Sharp said to all of us, "When I said there's no popping towels, I meant there's no popping towels!" Then he popped Albert's trembling bare behind with his paddle. Even the sound of it hurt! He hit Albert hard enough to bring tears. His body wobbled like long johns on the clothes line. The rest of us were dropped-jawed and silent. Still nobody breathed. I was dressed and ready for my next class.

"Now who else was popping towels with Pedrego?" Oh, that paddle wanted more! After a moment I squeaked, "Me. I was."

"Come here, Paul," Coach said. "Stand right here where Albert was standing." I was dressed, a new wallet well-positioned in my hip pocket. Without a word, *Whop!* Tears were down my face before the sound of it was done. *Oh! That! Hurt!* My knees went like wet spaghetti. I could not walk. I just stood there, quaking in electric pain.

"Paul, I hit you harder than I hit Albert because you already had your pants on. I'm sorry I made you boys cry, but when I said no popping towels, I meant it. Now is there anyone in here who still doesn't understand what I mean?" A loud silence echoed through that locker room. In front of everyone he respectfully said, "Paul, I appreciate you speaking up and being truthful."

Then, of all things, Tommy Owens spouted off. "He couldn't make me cry."

"What's that, Tommy?" Coach asked.

"I said you couldn't make me cry. I don't care how hard you hit me." Now Tommy Owens thought he was the toughest kid in Douglas, and he might have been, but he sure wasn't the smartest kid that day.

"Come over here, Owens!" Coach Sharp placed Tommy next to a support beam, one of those 4-inch steel beams that held up the ceiling. "Bend over and grab your ankles," he snorted. The paddle snorted, too. I'm convinced we heard adrenalin running through Coach. He spit into the palms of his hand and worked up a good two-handed grip on his paddle.

Owens smirked and dramatically leaned over and reached for his ankles. Coach Sharp positioned himself to let Tommy see a little of him. He waved a couple of bug-eyed boys out of the way and took up a batter's stance; paddle over his shoulder. He aimed a couple of controlled practice strokes at Owens' hind end. Then, with eyes blazing, he took a high step toward the far wall and with a mighty swing shattered his paddle against that steel beam.

"*Ba-yang-yang-yang!*"

Untouched, Tommy Owens fainted and fell over.

"*...yang-yang...*"

As far as I know, no one ever again popped towels in Coach Sharp's PE classes.

That *whop!* is not the only impact Coach Sharp had on me. I was never a school athlete, so he never coached me (although he umpired several of my Babe Ruth baseball games). I never took Drivers' Ed, so he never taught any of my classes. I sure learned a lot from him, though, and he left indelible imprints on me. First, he is a Christian man of the highest integrity. Second, despite his Arkansas roots, there isn't an ounce of prejudice within five hundred yards of Coach Sharp. Third, he is a motivator to one and all. Fourth, he's just Coach Sharp, and they just don't come any better.

The City of Douglas, the Douglas school system, the State of Arizona and almost thirty years of students are better because Coach Ike Sharp and his family lived in Douglas.

> *"Do not withhold discipline from a child;*
> *if you punish him with the rod, he will not die."*

— Proverbs 23:13

The Douglas High School Bulldogs

Always tall in our proud Black and Gold school colors, the great Douglas Bulldogs were notorious throughout Arizona. Not only did we beat you on the field, but we beat you up after the game, too. Sometimes, just for warm-ups, we beat you up under the bleachers during the game. (That's an editorial "we.")

Nobody liked the Douglas Bulldogs.

Throughout its history, Douglas High School boasted several state baseball championships, quite a few state track and field medals and great football respect. A state football championship? Close, but no cigar. What about basketball? Forget it.

● ● ●

Up-to-the-Minute Sports Department: Douglas can now boast two recent state soccer championships. It looks like DHS will be an Arizona high school soccer powerhouse for years to come. Go Dawgs!

● ● ●

I was a freshman (I think) when Douglas lost a close home football game to the Eloy Blue Devils. That spoiled an undefeated season and cost us our Number 1 state ranking. Everyone blamed the referees who made a controversial call with precious few seconds left in the game. A pack of angry adults attacked the referees, who scrambled over a ten-foot chain link fence to escape to their station wagon and high-tail it out of town, their civilian clothes still in the locker room.

Another bunch of adults harassed and threatened the Eloy football players. The tired team jumped on the bus without changing or showering and headed home. Those grown-ups chased them half way to Bisbee, throwing rocks at the bus the whole way.

It's the wild, wild west.

Rich fodder for the press. For two months Phoenix and Tucson newspapers ripped us hooligans down in Douglas. The end of it all was that Douglas High School was suspended from all athletic playoffs for two years. Nobody liked the Douglas Bulldogs.

•　•　•

Over the Years Department: I have heard, oh, a half dozen accounts of this incident from folks who lived in other Arizona cities. Talk about embellishment! To hear them tell it we did everything short of murder, torture and drowning of first born sons. Well, those stories sound great, but they just aren't true. But why spoil their fun? It's the wild, wild west.

•　•　•

The mother of all high school rivalries is between the great Douglas Bulldogs and the stinky Bisbee Pumas. It is the second oldest high school football rivalry in the US. The first game was played in 1906. We called those sissies the Bisbee Pumettes. I hated Bisbee High School. Can you think of anything uglier than red and gray? I hated Bisbee and anything or anybody associated with it.

THE GAME was the annual Douglas-Bisbee Thanksgiving Day football game. It was the last game of the season, the only day game and the only game that mattered. Just beat Bisbee and everything else will fall nicely into place. The prize, besides "bragging rights," is a handsome Copper Pick trophy, specially cast many years ago for this game only. The winning school got to keep it until it was wrested away another year.

But first came a week of frenzied preparation. We lit bonfires and dragged G Avenue for three nights, all the while singing our loyalty to Douglas High School.

We painted school spirit slogans on store windows along G Avenue. *"Beat Bisbee!!!" "Go Dawgs!" "Pound the Pumas!!!"*

We stationed guards around our D Hill to stop those Bisbee psychopaths from any attempt to befoul it.

"I just heard they're on their way to blow up the D!"

"Come on, everybody! Let's stop 'em!"

"Let's kill 'em, too!"

At school we hailed our mighty football team in one pep rally after another. Everybody got an A on science tests just to calm us down.

On Thanksgiving Day in Douglas and Bisbee the sun always shone brightly, hanging low in the southwest. The temperature was a pleasant 70-something degrees. A caravan of decorated cars rolled into the host town. Alumni from both schools filled the stadium. Townsfolk who attended no other games went to the Douglas-Bisbee game. A crowd of 7,000—even more—was common. Both marching bands outdid themselves at half time. Fights under the bleachers started about the middle of the third quarter. After the game, the police broke up the traditional fist fights in city parks next door to the stadiums, thus concluding the week's activities.

Those were great Thanksgiving weeks. My life and times at Douglas High School were a complete success because we beat Bisbee my senior year. (Again, an editorial "we." I didn't play.)

Not long after I graduated, some fuzzy-headed Arizona athletic rulers began a state playoff system and carved it into the long Thanksgiving weekend. Douglas doesn't beat Bisbee on Thanksgiving anymore. They do it earlier in the season now.

Unfortunately, during my years at DHS, we rarely fielded a respectable basketball team. To get even for its football losses BHS routinely thumped the Bulldogs two times a year. In fact, when I was a sophomore, I went up to Bisbee only to watch those Pumas plaster us 51 – 0 by the end of the first half. They laughed at us when the buzzer sounded.

Final score? *Holy cow!* – 16.

By the time I was a senior, my brother Neal was the new principal of Morenci High School. Morenci is a small copper-mining town a few hours north of Douglas. His Morenci Wildcats came to Douglas to bounce us Bulldogs all over the basketball court that year. For me, it was only a bittersweet loss, because in the end I got some "feel goods" about my brother's successful new career. Sort of. I haven't heard much about Morenci since then.

• • •

Oh, Now I Get It Department: Bisbee is one of the most delightful and picturesque cities in America. In the movie *L.A. Confidential*, Lynn Bracken (Kim Basinger) can hardly wait to get back to Bisbee. And who can blame her? Bisbee is in Cochise County, Arizona. It's the county seat, I'm proud to tell you. If I had grown up in Bisbee, I could have flipped everything in this story. I'll bet growing up there was almost as much fun as growing up in Douglas.

• • •

"Some men get the world. Some men get…a trip to Bisbee, Arizona."

—Lynn Bracken in *L.A. Confidential*

Four Easy Steps Through Douglas High School

Step One: Freshman year, Algebra I

In grades 3, 6, and 9, I was sick for three weeks at a time. Grade 3 we learned division. Grade 6 had something to do with long division and decimal points. Grade 9 was our introduction to Algebra. And I was out sick during the critical lessons when the foundation for each was laid. I played a frustrating game of math "catch-up" every day from third grade to graduation.

Everyone started high school (Ninth grade) in the Junior High building.

Step Two: Sophomore year, Algebra I again

We moved to the Douglas High School building(s) our Sophomore year. My favorite classes were English and anything to do with writing. I was part of the *Border Bulldog* staff, our school newspaper. I played on the junior varsity basketball team. I couldn't play on the baseball team because my grades went too low.

I was a good tenor in the A Cappella Choir; so good that I was selected to the Arizona All-State Choir two years in a row.

Step Three: Junior year, Algebra I (sigh)

I never did catch up with Sarah Sue Sparks in Typing I and II. We learned to type on green Olympia typewriters. All the keys were blank, so it didn't do us any good to look down to find a letter. When we reached 60 wpm we got to move up to brown IBM electric typewriters—still with blank keys. Sarah's flying fingers eventually topped more than 100 wpm. The best I ever did was only about 75 wpm. I think my sister Ruth typed as fast as Sarah by the time she finished high school.

I quit paying attention to World and US History. Same stuff; different books. Despite that, I had good grades in those classes. I enjoy history.

I liked Mrs. Hall, my English teacher. She lived in Bisbee (of all places) and drove down to Douglas. She was a battleaxe sometimes, but I enjoyed her and her classes.

Mr. Baysol Turner was my all-time favorite teacher. He taught journalism. He was a crusty old guy who put up with a lot of foolishness from us, but he drew the line at ungood writing. If we turned in something ungood, he made us rewrite till it was good, which for me was fun.

Jeanne Struthers nagged him pretty good one day about her side of a story. He got flustered and bellowed: "JEANNE! SHUT! UP!" The windows shook, then closed themselves. The whole class shut up. Jeanne shut up for the rest of the year.

Mr. Turner once let me bend some writing rules on a homework assignment. The words I wrote pranced around on that paper like *76 Trombones*. It was exciting. I read it over and over. I was the first one to class the next day. Mr. Turner read it, tapped his finger against my paper and almost spoke. He looked at it again, held up one finger and almost spoke again. Finally, he looked me in the eye and said, "Real good." When Mom read it after school, she flicked her eyebrows. I swaggered out to my room and called myself a writer. I have no idea now what I wrote then.

Front of Douglas High School. I took this photo on a Saturday morning with a Kodak Brownie camera. 1959 or 60.

Step Four: Senior year, Algebra I to the 4th Power

My four years in high school were either extremely average or really mediocre. I had a lot of fun in high school, but my senior year flew by way too quickly. I walked into school one day and walked out about a week later, it seemed. I dropped out of choir my senior year. I felt sorry for Joe Pinedo because I don't think Mr. Hyden, our third choir director, ever realized there was an All-State Choir. Joe deserved to go and I'm still upset that he didn't.

They let me be the Sports Editor of the *Border Bulldog* that year.

One hot, sultry afternoon, a few days before graduation, I was not paying attention in math class. "Paul?" I heard.

I snapped out of my daydream. "Yes, sir?" Mr. Sexton, my fourth Algebra I teacher, was leaning over his grade book.

"What year are you?"

"Senior."

Long stare. Long pause. Erase-erase. "I thought you were a junior," he mumbled. He brought my grade up to a D-minus.

• • •

Modern Schools Department: The trouble with today's schools is that teachers go ahead and pass their students whether they can do the work or not.

• • •

*"Don't worry about your difficulties in math.
I can assure you that mine are far greater."*

—Albert Einstein

189

Beer Cans Galore

I was cool one night at the big annual high school fair. Parents wandered from room to room while the boys in shop presented their pencil holders and bookends. I still envy a beautiful coffee table one boy made. I'll bet his parents are still proud of it. FFA boys showed off their cows and sheep and performed welding tricks. Home Ec girls displayed their hand-made potholders and baked fresh cookies for everyone.

The Girl's Chorus sang. The band played. The A Cappella Choir sang. I was in that choir. Mr. Wildung kindly introduced me as an up-and-coming local vocal talent. I sang a solo to a full auditorium. Did good, too. (Forgot the name of the song.) My parents were pretty proud and even told me so right there in the auditorium. A couple of girls thought I was good, too, and offered me flirtatious congratulations—just like in the movies. I was cool that night.

Mom and Dad gave me permission to go to the A&W Root Beer Drive-In for hamburgers with Joe Tippy, Joe Lerma and Joe Pinedo. Pinedo drove. Some of the fun of Douglas nights is "draggin' G Avenue." We made two or three passes up and down the avenue, but got bored when few others showed up. It was late, but much too early to go home.

We got the bright idea to make some noise at Hugh Bryant's house. Hugh Bryant was a relatively young police officer who never smiled. We thought his goal in life was to give every citizen of Douglas a ticket. So how to make some noise?

"Hey! Let's get some beer cans and toss them onto his porch. Wake him up!"

"That'll work. Let's do that!"

So we drove out on a dark connecting road near Pirtleville. That's where kids went to quaff underage beer. They tossed the empties along the road.

We gathered up beer cans galore. The back seat floor was so full we had to sit on our knees. Beer cans in the 50s were made of tin and made a lot more noise than aluminum ones.

We found the Bryant's house and we all pitched as many as possible onto his porch.

"Yee-haw!" *Clankety-clang!* "Yee-haw!" *Clankety-clang-clang!* That should wake him up!

Off we went, leaving a cloud of dust and noisy laughter behind. We were so cool. That was so much fun we decided to pelt the porch of Officer Al Rodriguez, too.

Clankety-clang! "Yee-haw!" *Clankety-clang-clang!* "Yee-haw!" That should wake him up, too!

"Who's next?"

"Fuller. Let's do Fuller's house!"

In the meantime, someone called the police, of all things. Before we got to Fuller's house, he was right behind us. He was a police officer, too, and was working that night. He spotted us eight blocks away, caught up with us and pulled us over on A Avenue. Uh-oh. He shined his big, long flashlight into the car. He paused to take a good look at all the remaining beer cans. "You boys been drinking?"

"No, sir."

"What're you doing with all those beer cans in the back seat?"

No comment.

"I want you boys to drive down to the police station. I'll be right behind you." We obeyed. Not a sound out of any of us.

One problem. We threw the cans on Bryant's *mother's* house, not his. She called the police. And so did Mrs. Rodriguez.

After the officers took our names and phone numbers, they got busy calling our parents. We didn't get arrested, but we sure got a good chewing out. "You stand right there till your parents get here. Don't say a word or I'll make you wait in a cell. You want that?"

"No, sir."

"I said, 'Don't say a word'!"

Boy, Dad was sure mad when he came down to get me at one o' clock in the morning. So was Pinedo's dad. So was Tippy's mother. And Lerma's dad. They were all mad!

When Dad and I left the police station, I saw Pinedo putting the rest of the beer cans into a trash can. His dad was standing over him, probably giving him "what for" for all the beer cans he hauled out of the back seat.

The next morning, a Saturday, my mom hauled me to Mrs. Bryant and to Mrs. Rodriguez and made me apologize. It was embarrassing.

We were required to go to Juvenile Court next week where we all stood before a lady judge. We waited—not cool, anymore—for her to throw the book at us. "If you boys were not drinking, then where did you get all those beer cans?" she asked.

"We picked them up along the highway."

"Really? You cleaned them up off the side of the road? Well, it sounds like you boys did a *good* thing. Picking up all that litter; keeping our roadsides clean. If only more people would do that. Well, since there wasn't any damage reported, I don't think there's a need to pursue this. But I don't want to see any of you boys in my courtroom again. Is that understood?

"*Yes, ma'am!*" (Four times.)

Outrage wasn't the word for it. Dad and Bryant and Rodriguez and Fuller were spitting nails. We four boys thought she was a cool judge.

That was not the only car stunt. More than once four or five of us boys climbed into the trunk of Dick Overfield's big Oldsmobile. We were very quiet while Dick drove us into the Cochise Drive-in Theater. We all gave Dick a quarter to cover the cost of his ticket. One time we got out of the trunk just as Anthony Perkins drove his knife into Janet Leigh in the Bates Motel shower stall. By the time we settled down, the movie wasn't scary. Not even when we paid full price a week later to see the whole show.

There came a time when some missing fence slats were our free gates into the drive-in. No wonder it went out of business.

• • •

Update Department: Officer Rodriguez and his family were great friends of my parents. He later became the mayor of Douglas.

• • •

"Your dad was the most indignant of them all."

—Joe Lerma, 2008

Joe and Joe and Dad and Mr. Jackson

One pleasant February afternoon after school, not long after my sixteenth birthday, I got involved with an interesting book. Dad interrupted me and asked if I wanted to go get my driver's license.

"I guess so," I said. He drove me to the testing place at the end of A Avenue where I took my written test and scored a perfect 100.

Mr. Irvin Bond then asked me if I wanted to drive or parallel park. I didn't know what parallel park meant, so I said I'd drive.

With four years of experience already under my belt I drove him around the block. No big deal. We returned to the office, he gave me a driver's license and told my dad, "Well, he can drive you home now."

Dad drove home and I went back to reading.

Mom sang, "Well, a perfect score. You must have studied pretty hard."

Studied? I didn't even know I was going to be tested.

When Joe Pinedo got his license, his dad bought him a light green Studebaker. To start it, he pushed the clutch in, which pushed the starter button on the floor. *Oooh! Neat!* After some months, a dark green, 1950 4-door Special Deluxe Plymouth replaced the Studebaker. His dad probably spotted a good deal and grabbed it. He was good at that. Mr. Pinedo was a premier mechanic at the Richfield gas station behind the Gadsden Hotel.

Joe was a nice guy. He offered to drive Joe Tippy and me to school every day. That was really convenient because we all were part of the early morning choirs. He also drove us to other school functions and took us home afterward if we asked him.

Pinedo was on the wrestling team. He was a solidly-built, rotund heavyweight. Hard to beat on a wrestling mat. Tippy was a thin, shy boy with a heart problem, so he wasn't allowed to participate in PE classes. He was a student librarian from the first day in high school. I'm sure he did a good job.

In our junior year, Mr. Jackson was our new choir director. He wore dirty white shirts to school and rolled the sleeves up to his biceps. He lived directly across the street from the school auditorium in the Coronado Courts, rental four-plexes.

We had an evening choir practice just before the Christmas concert. Joe took me and Joe, as was normal. Half way through practice, Mr. Jackson gave us a break while he ran across the street and grabbed a smoke.

Somehow, some way, during our horseplay, Joe Pinedo wrapped his huge arms around me from behind and lifted me up. Around and around he spun me. My arms were pinned to my sides.

"Okay, that's enough," I said.

He kept holding me.

"Come on, Joe. Put me down!"

He laughed and kept showing off in front of the choir kids.

"Joe! Let me down!" I fumed. He did. I whirled around and punched his grinning face.

"Fight! Fight!" They started yelling.

"[I called him a name]" I sneered.

"No wrestling! No wrestling!" someone was yelling. If we had wrestled, Joe would have crushed me like a paper cup. The choir was choosing sides and frantically encouraging both of us.

We traded a punch or two and—silly me—I looked into the noisy crowd for just one second.

Bam!

Joe's big fist plowed into my mouth. Blood spurted all over him. He split the inside of my lip, leaving a scar that is still visible.

Blood or no blood I swung back, just as Mr. Jackson pushed through the hollering crowd and stepped between us. It was a punch that went nowhere.

The break was over and we returned to the risers for more practice. It was quite a chore to stand there and sing with blood flowing out of my mouth, but Mr. Jackson had no sympathy for me. Afterward, I was still angry enough to walk home.

The next morning, Joe and Joe arrived on schedule to pick me up. I accepted the ride. He apologized, I apologized and we lived happily ever after.

Not long after that, Mr. Jackson kicked me out of the choir because "…you just won't blend in, will you?" Soon after that he called my parents and recommended that I attend a music camp in a faraway place called Upstate, New York. My dad had a lengthy conversation with Mr. Jackson about getting back into the choir immediately, and "Let's see how he does at All-State this year before we think about sending him off to summer camp." I dutifully went back to choir a week after I got kicked out.

Joe and I had a friendly competition between us to earn the trip to Arizona All-State Choir that year. He had a more powerful tenor voice than I did. I was convinced Mr. Jackson would choose him to go. No, I went. But I knew in my heart that Joe deserved it.

I never told Joe about the phone conversation I overheard between Dad and Mr. Jackson. I never went to Upstate, New York, either.

• • •

Last Laugh Department: Joe Pinedo became a well-known opera tenor. He performed with several big city opera companies and worked alongside the great tenors, Plácido Domingo and Luciano Pavarotti. It doesn't get any better than that. God bless him.

• • •

"Dear friend, I pray that you may enjoy good health and that all may go well with you…"

—3 John 1:2

D Day

Douglas High School doesn't have homecoming. Instead, we celebrate D Day.

All week prior to D Day, the new sophomores (freshmen, beginning in 1960) were initiated into DHS. They carried seniors' books, yelled "Hail, Senior!" and made other humiliating noises. I heard that some underclassmen got beaten up by upperclassmen during that week. Hmmm. One senior held his foot on my back while I did a few pushups for him. Classrooms and class times were off limits for initiation. Thank goodness. I thought initiation was corny. Even when I was a senior I sort of ignored it. But Mr. Beedle said, "...and some kids had a great time this week. Doesn't matter what class they're in."

D Hill. Photo taken at Christmastime, 1970. Mike, Marcie and me, standing about 100 yards below the bottom of the D. Dad took this picture.

In Douglas, two days before D Day, the senior boys wait for the sophomore boys up on D Hill. There's an old broom for everyone, empty coffee cans, rags, several barrels of kerosene, and several barrels of whitewash. It's always a hot October afternoon.

When the school bus unloads, our D gets a fresh coat of whitewash from the proud sophomore boys. From the top of the D, you cannot see its bottom, and vice versa. It's a huge D, and takes all the sophomores available to get it cleaned up in just half a day. The seniors enthusiastically encourage them with taunts, threats, name-calling, bullying and other verbal acts of terrorism. If that doesn't work, then a few whacks with belts or ocotillo branches are effective.

Sometimes the passion reaches such a fever pitch that a sophomore boy or two will enthusiastically answer in kind. It's a good thing that a few adult teachers are there to...uh, separate the gusto. Did Julian Smith really use an electric cattle prod?

Even the steep hill gets involved. It is an effort to walk from the top of the D to the bottom without falling down. Getting back to the top almost requires walking on all fours. Otherwise, you'll lose your balance and...well, you really don't want to lose your balance on D Hill. The rocks are not little pieces of pea gravel, either. The smallest one is probably the size of a football. When all those boys get up there and start sweating together, gnats and flies show up. Snakes are no problem because with two hundred teenage boys up there making a bunch of racket, the snakes hurry away.

The coffee cans are stuffed with rags that were well-soaked in that kerosene. Then they're tucked among the clean, whitewashed rocks. When we're done, hundreds of cans fill the D. Tired boys go home from school that evening, licking wounded egos and asking Mama to mend their blisters.

This honorable chore, completed year after year, is the very blood and heart of the Douglas High School Bulldogs. The girls and junior students who remained on campus that day did so with respect and reverence. The next morning, when those sophomore boys look up at D Hill from town—five miles away—the D is remarkably clean and white. They always do a good job, and their egos are strong again.

Then that night, the night before D Day, we burned every box in Cochise County. The bonfire shot sparks two hundred feet in the air while we all gathered around and sang *"Douglas High School, hats off to thee..."*

198

D Day. 8:00 at night. Immediately after the D Day football game kick-off, the PA announcer informed everyone, "Ladies and Gentlemen. The D is lit." [*Roar from the crowd!*]

Of all the events in Douglas, lighting the D is the most impressive. Student fans crane their necks or run up to the top of the bleachers. The band plays *"We're loyal to you, Douglas High..."* Alumni who come home wipe at little tears and yell, "Alright, go get 'em, Bulldogs!" Proud parents peek and pretend that it's no big deal. "It's beautiful, isn't it?"

It is a big deal.

"Oooh. Aaah." You can see it all the way to Bisbee. It glows during the game and well after the dance. When everyone in town finally goes to sleep, the D quietly burns out.

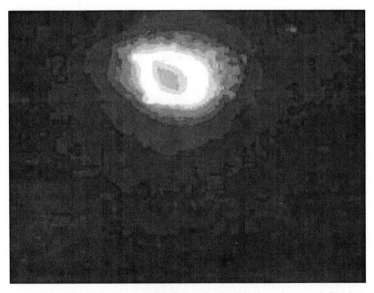

An elegant Golden D proudly floats in the black Arizona night sky. Black and Gold.

DHS History Department: Our first D Day was in 1933. At the big pep rally the night before that first special game, the captain of the football team vowed that the Douglas High School Bulldogs "...will never lose a D Day game." After five consecutive wins, other schools challenged the Bulldogs for that D Day game, only to go home whipped each time. The meanest team in El Paso, the Ysleta High School Indians, foolishly challenged all the way from Texas. The Bulldogs made quick work of them. It's a long, hot ride home after a loss to Douglas.

Alas, after thirteen consecutive D Day victories, Glendale Union High School figured out a way to win in Douglas on D Day. When I was in high school, we won all our D Day games.

• • •

"Once a Bulldog...always a Bulldog."

—DHS Alumni

First at Douglas High School

Neal First

My brother Neal was our family's first DHS graduate in 1951. Then Noel in '54, myself in '61, and Ruth in '64. By the way, the first graduating class from the new Douglas High School buildings on Fifteenth Street was the Class of 1950. Prior to that for many years, DHS was on Twelfth Street where I went to junior high school.

First Classmates

Many years after I graduated from high school, I met up with Jeanne Struthers. We visited for four hours one Saturday. I wouldn't trade that afternoon for anything. Anyway, we agreed that everyone in our DHS graduating class was family. After all, we first started out in Kindergarten together and ended up graduating together. We knew where everyone lived and where their parents worked. We knew most of their brothers and sisters. We knew who went to which church— who didn't go to church. We knew what grades were received. We knew who were best friends and who didn't like one another. We knew all about each other. Sometimes too much. We really were family—we just grew up together in different houses.

First Dancers

After every home football and basketball game, we sock-hopped till midnight. Kay Yotty was a good friend of mine from church. She was a tiny thing and she sure knew how to dance! She and I had the whole dance floor to ourselves one night with a big crowd around us because in Douglas we were the first couple to do The Twist.

By the way, Kay married a fundamentalist preacher and, knowing what I do about fundamentalist preachers, I'm willing to bet that they still haven't had their own first dance.

Me First

Every year, graduating seniors gave an appreciation gift to the high school. A little plaque was usually attached.

Our Class of '61 had no money, so buying any benches or flagpoles or new sidewalks—or even a plaque—was out of the question.

Well, DHS had two robust fight songs, but no Alma Mater. Who ever heard of a great school with no Alma Mater? So our gift to Douglas High School was its Alma Mater, a real pretty song, too.

I am the one who sang it first to an all-school assembly. [*Rousing round of applause—whistle, whistle.*]

"Alright! Now everybody stand up and *sing it...!*"

"You did a good job this morning, Paul. Proud of you."

—Coach Ike Sharp, May 1961

G Avenue

There are four delightful places in Douglas that aren't on Seventh Street. One is Agua Prieta across the line. Then there's Douglas High School on Fifteenth Street, and the First Baptist Church at Tenth and E. And fourth, G Avenue on G Avenue. It's the main business street. If you follow it north, it will bend and lead you to Bisbee. If you follow it south, you will crash into that fence that divides the US and Mexico.

When I was little, G Avenue was "downtown." I tagged along with Dad to get something at Posten's Hardware store or pick up a prescription at Arizona Drug. Mom always took us along to S.H. Kress or Newberry's, the dime stores with powerful popcorn aromas that swooned everyone who entered. Shopping at Levy's always meant a new pair of P. F. Flyers. Not long after Thanksgiving, most of the stores along G Avenue put dreamy Christmas displays in the windows.

G Avenue in Douglas; looking south. This intersection at Twelfth and G is just twelve blocks from the Mexican Border.

Every front door on G Avenue had a distinct, squeaking sound when it opened. If it didn't squeak, then a little bell tinkled. Squeaky floors were tongue and groove wood. The first automatic door I ever saw was in Tucson.

"Mornin', Mr. Nichols."

"Howdy. Came in for a new flashlight battery." (If a lady clerk greeted him, he tipped his hat as well.)

"A new one, eh? Just one all you need?"

"Well, let me look at that thing first." And Dad studiously examined the new flashlight battery. Hefted it. Checked both ends. "That's the one. I believe that'll be all, thank you. How much you want? Twenty cents?"

"That'll be twenty-one cents, please."

"Twenty-one cen…oh, that's right: the governor has to get his fingers in the pie, too, doesn't he?"

"Them taxes is killin' us, ain't they?"

We watched all parades on G Avenue. When I was little, I almost always stood on a certain fire hydrant and held on to a nearby light pole. That was a good spot, but I had to get there early ahead of some other boy my size. When I was about seven, Percy the big policeman, set me on his shoulders once while a western-theme float went by.

When I got older, the favorite place on G Avenue was the Douglas Drug store, where all the teeny-boppers hung out on Saturday. They served the best hamburgers in the history of mankind. Terrific tacos, too. We played nickel pinball machines in the Valley News and Curio Store. We just called it the Newsstand. Frank Fair's Sport Shop, the shop that sponsored my Little League team, was a favorite place even if you didn't buy anything.

I was embarrassed in there one day. My first day in junior high, Coach Sharp told us a jock strap was required for PE. "Go get one. You can get them at Fair's." Jock straps had a different name, but try as I might, I couldn't remember what it was.

Wouldn't you know it, two pretty high school clerks waited on me. While I shuffled around, mumbled and hoped Mr. Fair would show up, they guessed why I was there. "Is this what you want? A supporter for PE?"

Next door to Fairs, the B&P Pool Hall and Tavern was open to anyone who could see over the top of a pool table. No drinking until age twenty-one, but if you had the money, they let you shoot pool. Fifteen cents a game. There were five busy pool tables and one snooker table. A thin, old man gathered and racked the balls for every new game. We entered and exited through the back door, against the alley. I learned to shoot pool in there—the hard way. Everybody else was better than me.

When we got our driver's licenses and when our folks let us use the car, we dragged G. "Draggin' G" meant driving from Eighth Street to Thirteenth Street, then making a U-turn to do it again and again. It was best to have a several friends in the car with you. Somewhere along the way, passengers spotted friends in another car. "Hey! Lemme out!" A quick exchange of passengers was made in the middle of the street, which created a four-car gridlock.

An older boy I knew, Mike Molina, had a beautiful, customized Mercury with scallops in the hood and flames on the side. Donnie Woodall had a '51 Ford, custom painted dark blue and white. His seats were custom white and blue tuck-n-roll. Those two dragged G longer than all the others, just showing off their pretty cars.

After six or eight drags, we stopped to hang out in the Pioneer Café and plunk nickels into tabletop jukeboxes. Hanging out at the Pioneer Café was somewhat like the Saturday afternoon matinees— trading seats was part of the decorum, unless you had a date.

For every home football game, the merchants on G Avenue let the high school students paint black and gold slogans on the big plate glass windows, urging the Bulldogs on to victory. On Saturday morning, we had to go back and wash it all off.

After a football victory, everybody squeezed into a car to drag G. We honked horns and screamed verbal graffiti for twenty minutes, then drove back to the high school cafeteria for the dance. After that we drove back to the Pioneer Café for hamburgers.

When we were on G Avenue, our parents never worried about us—much. It's a nice place.

"The chariots storm through the streets, rushing back and forth through the squares. They look like flaming torches; they dart about like lightning."

—Nahum 2:4

The Joy of Color

Besides the people I've already mentioned, there are a few more that opened the doors of my life or climbed through a window of my heart and stayed.

Beverly Morgan, our pastor's oldest daughter, is the best example. I knew her about five years. She played the piano for me every time I sang. She was not only an accompanist, but a coach and motivator, too. We loved each other like nobody's business. We never said so, but we knew. She dated Tom Richardson for several months, but her heart was always with me. We were deep, deep friends. I thought so, anyway.

It was a tough night the night before the Morgans left town. It was the Sunday night following my high school graduation. Beverly had already left for college, but was home for the summer. Well, not really. Douglas wasn't home for the Morgans any longer. Pastor Morgan had decided to move his family to Hawaii. Beverly and I drove up to D Hill for her to look down on the beautiful Douglas lights one last time. It was our first and only date. We didn't say much. She sat close to me and cried. I just stared out the window, thinking, "Dad-gum it." The abrupt move by her dad was painful for the whole congregation—and for his family. Everybody thought he made the wrong decision.

Slowly, slowly, I drove Beverly home. I walked her to the front door where we hugged for a long time. I walked away lonely and empty. I slammed their wrought iron front gate with everything I had. The Morgans left town the next day, and I haven't seen Beverly since. I don't know where she went, but she never left.

Pastor Morgan definitely made the wrong decision.

Sharon Utke was born just four days before me on Groundhog Day. Our moms shared the same hospital room for a day or two. We were pals and friends K-12. She was always the tallest girl in our class. She was always the smartest girl in our class. Not only that, but she was the classiest girl in our class, too. She didn't walk, she floated. From way back in first grade she carried herself with grace and charm.

One day in the seventh grade I happened to look down at her. I looked *down* at her. But I always looked up to her.

Jon and **Lisa Long,** twin brother and sister. Again K-12. I played at their house many times.

Rene Friend is the first person I ever really felt sorry for. His family moved from Mexico to Douglas and he was deposited into our third grade class. He only spoke Spanish. I guess it was up to him to learn English any way he could. There were no tutors or ESL classes. The only English word he knew was his own last name. I liked him and tried to communicate a little. I didn't get very far, but I tried. It wasn't fair for him to have to fend for himself like that. Luis Rodriguez and Elda Cuellar helped him some. First chance I got, I chose him for my kickball team during recess. He was quiet all the time and made poor grades. But he showed up when we started the fourth grade. And the fifth grade. I remember the first time I ever saw him raise his hand to volunteer an answer. I was impressed. He done good. He learned English and got along just fine after that. And he did it all on his own, as far as I know. If only I was half as good with my Spanish. Rene graduated with us and I should have told him I admired his accomplishment.

Les Stimac peddled Popsicles and ice cream goodies on a bicycle about the time we were thirteen or so. A year or two later his dad helped him get a three-wheeled, motorized Cushman ice cream truck. By the time he left high school he had a fleet of two of them. Les was popular at school and a cut-up from the get-go. He always found the humorous side of everything and gleefully passed it on to the rest of us. After I got married, Les and his wife Pat Brown, who's also from Douglas, became quite close with me and Gloria even though they lived in California and we lived in Phoenix.

Charlie Ables, Steve Geshell, John Crum, Billy Taylor, Tom Kenyon, Bobby Mathay and a bunch of other white, protestant boys like me were all members of DeMolay, a Masonic white, protestant, youth organization, with a secret handshake and everything. At the time I didn't realize I was an official racist, but I'm far from the Masons now. We didn't know it at the time, but Les Stimac wasn't allowed to join us because he was Catholic.

Harley and **Charlie Marquis** had such poor eyesight that they held everything they read about two inches away from their thick, thick glasses. They made great grades in school, though. They didn't participate in PE, art and so forth, because they couldn't see very good. They were rarely apart. If you saw one, you saw the other. They were good and loyal friends to everyone. Their deaths occurred within months of each other. Nobody didn't like Harley and Charlie, identical twin brothers.

Edmond Lewis and I shared the same bed when we went to All-State Choir our junior year. It was the only one available. On the bus trip up there, he beckoned me to his seat and barely whispered, "Are there any coloreds in the choir?" It was the same weekend that the Little Rock, Arkansas, high school was desegregated. That weekend we listened to radio reports during lunch, and walked silently together, each of us trying to figure out…

A few days later, there was Edmond with some other students; cutting up, laughing, having a good time in front of the DHS bell tower. I stared at him long and hard. Edmond was the most popular student in our school. He was fun and full of life. He was both inspirational and motivational to all of us white students. While I stared at him and recalled those radio diatribes from Little Rock, I wondered if he had a deep and empty hole in his heart. I hope the little friendship I gave him is acceptable.

Edmond Lewis, Eunice Peevey, Rene Friend and **Gloria Amaya** introduced me to the Joy of Color and I love them every one. God bless them all.

Willard Henry—I've been told that every town has a "town idiot." I was ours sometimes, but the man during the 40s and 50s was Willard Henry. I'm not writing to make fun of him. It's just that every town has it own colorful character.

Willard was a tallish man, about forty. He was far and away the most bow-legged person I ever saw. He was born with mental and physical defects. He was about four years old upstairs, possibly younger. Bowed legs was one of his defects. He lived with his widowed mother somewhere over on Eighth Street. Most of the times

I saw him he was staggering up or down G Avenue talking loudly to himself, or to a parking meter, wearing Gene Autry's dirty hat.

Willard wore western clothes; not Levi's, but dirty, western-cut slacks. He wore the same clothes for days and weeks on end. He only had one hat: Gene Autry's. His shirt pockets and all his pants pockets bulged with who knows what, including a pair of tweezers.

I sat next to him at the Walgreen Drug Store one Saturday morning when I was twelve. We were the only two at the counter for awhile, sitting on round stools, elbows on the marble countertop, drinking Cherry 7-Ups. He mumbled constantly, quietly. We didn't speak to each other. I twisted back and forth on my stool and I took a good look at him, thinking it might be a good idea to remember this man. Willard smelled bad.

His graying beard was about a quarter of an inch long. Close to his ear, it was much longer. Same thing at the corners of his mouth. I heard that his mom shaved him. One of his eyes was noticeably larger than the other and he breathed loudly through his nose. His soft, bony hands shook when he picked up his drink, and he had a hard time aiming the straw at his mouth. He emptied his shirt pockets and reviewed their contents, then put everything back. He did that about three times. He had little wads of paper, bobby pins, dirty old business cards, a stubby pencil, bottle caps, coins…an amazing assortment of little things. Occasionally he looked over in my direction, but our eyes never met. I noticed the lady behind the soda counter didn't charge him for his drink.

High school boys teased Willard when they spotted him on G Avenue. Maybe they deliberately bumped into him and shoved him. Worse, they shouted, "Gene Autry doesn't like you anymore, Willard!" Then, in a shrill, high-pitched voice with no compare, he blathered curses at them till he finally staggered to the end of the block. He used every known foul word in both English and Spanish. Where did he learn all those dirty words? A few shop owners rushed out to quiet him down. That was futile, because Willard woke up G Avenue from the underpass on Fifteenth Street clear down to the Complete Auto Supply store on Seventh Street. The teasing boys hot-footed it out of sight, laughing all the way.

One day, long before I was born, Gene Autry, "The Singing Cowboy," came to town for an afternoon school concert in the old high school auditorium. Somehow, Willard Henry got backstage during the concert. Just wandering around like any curious four-year-old, I guess. Anyway, a couple of ornery boys pushed him through the curtains out onto the stage with Gene Autry. The audience loved it. Hoo-haw! *Hoo-haw!*

Gene Autry didn't. He immediately recognized the situation. He put his arm around the embarrassed and terribly confused Willard, and said (words to the effect), "This is my friend. I'm glad he's up here on stage with me." He turned to Willard and said, "Here, you can wear my cowboy hat. [Plunked it on his head.] And you stay right here with me while I sing the rest of my songs."

The audience went silent, ashamed. Willard was the talk of the town—as usual.

John Slaughter, Pancho Villa, Gene Autry, Rex Allen and Willard Henry are a few of the colorful cowboys who helped shape Douglas. They're a great bunch of characters who helped shape me, too.

Another bunch of characters are my high school friends.

"For the sake of my brothers and friends, I will say,
'Peace be within you'."

—Psalm 122:8

Graduation Ceremonies at Douglas High School

Douglas High School's annual graduations are held outside in the football stadium. When all was said and done for the Class of 1961, I danced and hugged with 208 ecstatic grads. Our parents and teachers were even happier. There was just one thing left to do: return my cap and gown. I muscled my way into the gleeful crowd, tossed my stuff into a box—and suddenly I was never more alone in all my life.

> *". . .for I know the plans I have for you," declares the Lord,*
> *"plans to prosper you and not to harm you,*
> *plans to give you a hope and a future."*
>
> —Jeremiah 29:11

(I didn't live at 1122 Seventh Street when I graduated from high school, but I want to include this bit of information.)

Mrs. Nichols

At Mom's funeral, when Mike Foster was forty-something, he told me, "I never knew your mother's name was Nell till I saw her obituary. To me, she was always just Mrs. Nichols."

Mom, mid-1950s.

And that's exactly how she wanted it. From the moment she said "I do!" she was Mrs. Nichols and nothing else. The only time she used her first name was on legal documents. I never heard my dad call her by name. And that'll be the day when someone younger will call her by her first name.

One day I drove Mom into the Neatest Driveway on Earth, pulled back on the steering wheel and said, "Whoa, Nellie." I got backhanded.

The story goes that when she was in high school, a neighbor gave her a ride on his buckboard (about 1920 BC—Before Cars). After she politely thanked him for the ride and stepped down, the man snapped the horse's reins and snapped, "Git up there, Nellie!" Mom snapped around thinking he was being fresh with her. He's lucky he didn't get backhanded. Don't compare her with a horse.

Another story goes that I introduced Mom to a thirty-year-old wannabe hippie friend who quickly asked, "And what is your first name?" Mom sputtered something, but nothing sensible came out. I quickly shouted, "Missus!" so my friend wouldn't get backhanded.

I never knew a better Bible teacher than my own mother. My niece Debbie thinks so, too. Mom taught a women's Bible class at church all the years I lived in Douglas—and then some. Many is the night that Mom lay on her bed reading her Bible or lessons or commentaries or all of the above. She lay there reading and eating saltine crackers or nuts or grapes or Sugar Crisps or all of the above. She studied at the dining room table, too, with reference books piled high, a bowl of grapes beside them. She kept her lesson notes in little three-ring notebooks. Some of those note binders are now in our basement storage. Someday they might come in handy. She wrote sermon notes along the edges of her Bible pages and in minute white spaces between chapters. It got to the point where you couldn't read the text.

Our mom was a stay-at-home mom before there ever was such a term. All the moms I knew were stay-at-home moms. In our neighborhood all the moms watched out for all the kids. All the moms knew all the other mom's rules, too—and helped enforce them.

"Richie, does your mother know you're shooting a BB gun at the street light?"

But you know what? Mrs. De la Vara and Eleanor Foster and Mrs. Haro and all the rest of them cared about me and Ruth. And Mom cared about their kids. They cared just enough to make sure we didn't send ourselves to the hospital or to jail. I'll bet they all breathed a great sigh of relief when we finally left home for good.

"Paul, will you go get me some tortillas, please?" Mom gave me three dimes. I hopped on my bike and hurried to the tortilla factory about three blocks down Seventh Street. It smelled so great in there. That was my favorite errand.

"Hola, Pablito."

"Hi, *yo quiero tres docena tortillas de maiz, por favor.*" I got to watch all thirty-six corn tortillas fall out of the little press. They were hot to the touch. Once in awhile the nice Mexican lady gave me an extra one to eat right there. They were so good they buckled my knees. Mom fixed tacos and enchiladas better than any Anglo I ever met. Lucky me: she taught my bride, who had never eaten a taco till I married her and took her home to meet my parents. All my life I've eaten world class tacos and enchiladas at my own dinner table.

Mrs. Nichols was a beautiful young woman who passed her good looks on to the rest of us. But she ate too many snacks in bed and enjoyed too much of her own good cooking. She spent most of her last thirty years dieting.

Now besides Dad, there was another special man in Mom's life. The man really liked Mom and she was always glad to see him. He came to the house at least once a month, sometimes more. The Fuller Brush Man brought his samples and little catalogs, and Mom carefully reviewed each page. She dutifully watched his amazing demonstration, then ordered that product whether she needed it or not. It was usually on sale.

"And then I'll take one of these here on page twelve."

"Okay. Anything else?"

"And let me have one of these on page sixteen."

"You're in luck, Mrs. Nichols. That's on special this month."

"It is? Well, let me have six of them then."

"Yes, ma'am. And oh, this item right across the page," he pointed out, "is on sale this month, too."

"Well, good. Let me have six of those, too. What else is on sale?" Mom nearly went broke saving money with the Fuller Brush man. He really liked Mom. Over the years, Mom never a met a Fuller Brush man she didn't like.

And she never met a telephone she didn't like, either. Phone conversations with June Richardson lasted half the morning. Our only phone was on the end table next to the couch. It sat atop the Nichols family guest book. Every day Mom curled up there and chatted away with June as if they hadn't talked to each other for weeks. I was such an ornery squirt. When she got on the phone, I took a bite of a banana, ran into the living room and asked if it was okay to have it. She always nodded and waved me on. When Dad was at work, he always called her about mid-shift just to see how she was doing.

When Ruth and I were old enough to fend for ourselves in an empty house, Mom took a part-time job as a telephone operator. The kind that said, "Number, please." What a perfect job. She got to talk on the phone and get paid, too. Ruth and I had to be careful about using the phone then, because if Mom was the operator who answered we had to have a good reason for being on the phone. We didn't think it was fair for Mom to be at home when she was at work. Just about a year later the telephone company gave everybody a dial telephone and sent the operators home.

Then she became the full time cashier at J. C. Penney down on Tenth Street and F Avenue. She sat upstairs making change. When a customer paid for a purchase, the money was put into a canister and sent up to Mom through a hydraulic tube. Mom made change and sent the canister back. Before those tubes, the money was put into the canister and hooked to a cable. The clerk pulled a chain and the little container went zinging over the heads of everyone, up to Mom. She zang it back down the cable with the change in it.

She used a Monroe Calculator, a huge adding machine, to do her bookkeeping. But first she did it all in her head, then reluctantly used the Comptometer to prove that she was right. Only once did I ever hear her fret about not balancing her daily till—for just a few pennies. One day after school, she and her boss introduced me to Mr. J. C. Penney up there in her office. He scruffed my hair.

When Mom started working she only had to sacrifice one thing: half-day phone chats with June Richardson. When Mom started working, Ruth and I had to have all our chores done by the time she got home—or else. Ruth usually got hers done. I frequently got or else.

Her income was converted into a new refrigerator and lots more socks for me and Ruth. I suppose she earned about sixty-five cents an hour when she first started working. That didn't matter: she proudly gave it everything she had.

Mom was born in a log cabin somewhere in the Tennessee mountains. Her father's name is Thomas Wilbur Shaw. Uncle Lewis and Aunt Crosie are her brother and sister. That's all I know about her side of the family. That's sad.

But look who all Mrs. Nichols left behind!

•   •   •

Update Department: In his diaries, Dad refers to Mom as "Nell" every time. Except once he called her "the wife."

•   •   •

"May your father and mother be glad;
may she who gave you birth rejoice!"

—Proverbs 23:25

Nick

"Tucson, Aug 1 – '31 Taking oath of office and getting sworn in. Issued gun #27533 Badge #1173"

—The first entry in Dad's diary.

He was a handsome man with dashing silver-white hair. In my eyes Dad was an Immigration officer, a beekeeper, a pillar in our church—not always in that order.

Dad, mid-1950s.

In his own eyes he was a railroad man from the get-go. He worked for the Southern Pacific Railroad for a few years after he and Mom got married, but was laid off during the Depression. He had a few heartbreaks in his life and that was one of them. Fortunately, the

217

Border Patrol was looking for some new Border Patrolmen at the time. He wasn't out of work for long.

In Mom's eyes he was Nick. The love of her life. He could do no wrong. The first time Dad saw Mom he looked back to see if she was looking back to see if he was looking back to see if she was looking back at him. She was.

When he first started, he patrolled the US–Mexico border on horseback between El Paso, Texas, and Nogales, Arizona. He had a tent that he packed along for the nights he slept in the desert. And a .45 pistol. And dynamite sticks. And a rifle of some kind. I doubt if he ever fired them in the line of duty. But I heard he and his buddies occasionally stuck dynamite into Saguaro cacti and blew them up just to watch them go all to pieces. He oughta be arrested!

After a few years he became an Immigration Officer and it was his great joy to "…cut some of that red tape" to help a Mexican obtain a visa. He enjoyed his job, especially interacting with people who came and went across the line.

Practical jokes were his pastime there at work. His favorite: occasionally sassy Mr. Businessman from another state made a tourist trip into Mexico. Just to be on the safe side, he left his valuables checked at the Port—cameras included. Pretty soon a pretty Mexican girl came walking into the US. Dad complimented her beauty and asked to take her picture. "Oh, si!" she eagerly agreed. So Dad took the man's camera and clicked off two or three smiling poses.

And what do you suppose Mr. Businessman explained to his wife when he got back home?

Dad studied fingerprints during his working hours. He rolled many a Mexican finger over fingerprint cards. So many that he became something of an expert. Every so often he entertained someone at our house with all the ins and outs of whorls, arches and loops—our fingerprint designs. He knew what he was talking about, too; enough so that he was subpoenaed to several trials in Tucson to testify as an expert witness.

Dad at work at the Port. Picture taken late 1950s.

No one ever visited our house without Dad taking them to Our Back Yard to see his bees. He took you out there and brought you back with a quart jar of honey. Free! He always turned the honey jar upside down, pointed out the large air bubble and said, "You get a free balloon, too."

When it was time to extract honey he always opened the garage door to any neighborhood boy or girl who wanted to watch. He let them poke their noses into all manner of things. He let them turn the extractor crank. He let them open the spout to pour out fresh honey. And he let them eat all the honeycomb they wanted. Once in awhile, he whacked off a couple of chunks of honeycomb and sent it home with a kid.

When our church doors opened, Dad was there. Many times he was there when the doors weren't open. He loved his church. On the night of his funeral Mom told me, "There was nothing he would rather do than take up the offering." That's almost right.

In the First Baptist Church of Douglas, Dad

- faithfully cranked out about 100 bulletins every week for many years;
- faithfully served as a deacon for many years;
- was the church treasurer for a couple of spells;
- was Chairman of the Board of Trustees a time or two;
- faithfully taught a men's Sunday School class all the years I lived in Douglas;
- as a master of *Robert's Rules of Order*, moderated most business meetings;
- performed a lot of physical labor to help maintain the church building and the parsonage next door;
- faithfully drove widows to church, sometime making two trips;
- and he took up the offering for many years, just like Mom said.

That was just at our church. Dad also

- helped establish the new Southern Baptist Church in Douglas even though he had no intention of ever being part of it. A competing church, if you will.
- opened his home to overnight missionaries and ministers for many years;
- served in, donated to and participated in Agua Prieta churches for many years: *Iglesia Bautista* and *Iglesia Asamblios de Dios*;
- financially supported missionaries in Africa, Mexico, the Far East, South America and the US (not counting what he put in the church offering plate).

That's a short list of Dad's loving, sacrificial service to the Lord. Neal and Ruth can probably add more. His Christian service has trickled down all the way to his great-grandchildren.

Sometimes while ushering, just to be ornery, he took the offering plate from someone on the end of the pew and then whispered something like, "Hey, come on...how 'bout a little more than that?" He held the plate there for a few seconds, waiting for more offering. Then he winked, smiled and moved on—much to the comic relief of his victim.

When I was a junior in high school, Pastor Morgan read his resignation at the end of a morning service. A corporate gasp echoed through the sanctuary. He just broke several hearts. Earlier, before church, he called my dad aside, broke the news to him alone and then asked him to say the closing prayer. While he prayed, Dad jangled the change in his pocket and cried.

There's much more to Dad. He loved classic poetry and the *National Geographic*. He knew the names of a heaven's worth of desert stars. He was a misplaced railroad machinist who yearned to return, but figured it was "...best to grow where I'm planted." Dad never threw much away. Anything that remotely had a vague use someday went into a can or a box or an old tub or on a shelf. Even our garbage was plowed into his garden. He enjoyed good music—except Rock 'n' Roll.

Dad had only one flaw: he never took us fishing.

About the middle of the '50s he discovered the 35mm camera. It wasn't long before he was an accomplished photographer, clicking off some of the best desert scenes, sunsets and lightning flashes you ever saw. He sold a few photos to magazines and left behind several thousand.

He kept a diary from way back in August 1931, his first day on the job with the Border Patrol. He recorded daily activities with precious little commentary or emotion. Neal has them all now.

"January 25, 1981. Noel Quentin Nichols died today."

—The last entry in Dad's Diary

The Beautiful and Historical First Baptist Church

I was born on a Saturday night and eight days later I was in the house of the Lord for the first time (no, I'm not Jewish). I rarely missed a Sunday after that—even after I left home. Mom and Dad made sure of that. Neal, Noel and Ruth had an identical start to their lives.

When I think of our church, people come to mind and I can easily recall a bunch of them. Four stand out: Pastor Morgan and his daughter Beverly, Mr. Martin who taught me my firm handshake, and Mr. Dawson, the janitor who dipped snuff. Not to mention lots of kids. And, mind you, there are plenty more adults I can list.

Isn't that the way it's supposed to be when we think of the Lord's house? People, not buildings?

Nevertheless, the First Baptist Church is a beautiful building, inside and out. A sterling white building with a dainty chapel off to one side. The sanctuary and chapel are connected by a thirty foot breezeway of Mexican-influenced architecture. I believe the chapel was the original sanctuary. Behind that breezeway was a grassy courtyard where teens courted and restless young boys wrestled. Every Spring, colored eggs lay exposed for all the little children to find.

In the sanctuary, some architect did a masterful job of placing exposed roof beams. A gorgeous stained-glass window decorates the rear of the sanctuary. Up front a back-lighted, stained-glass mural of Christ in Gethsemane watches over the podium. On the pulpit is a permanent little plaque addressed to whoever's speaking. "GENTLEMEN, WE WOULD SEE JESUS," it says. The First Baptist Church is a lovely place to worship. I was too young and too close to it to appreciate its beauty.

First Baptist Church, Douglas, Arizona. Dad took this picture, mid-1950s.

On the same city block are the Methodist, Episcopal and Presbyterian churches, each on its own corner. They're beautiful buildings, too. Solid early-century buildings; each thoughtfully and elegantly built for praise and worship. The block was donated by the Phelps-Dodge Corporation way back when Douglas was about a year old. The only stipulation is that if the churches stop being churches, then P-D gets the land back. *Ripley's Believe It or Not* once noted that this is the only city block in the world with a church on every corner. Designating that block as a national historical site is a great idea, if you ask me. I think it's an Arizona historical site, if that counts.

When I was in junior high school, it was an easy two-block walk to the church. Every Monday after school, it was my service to change the outside marquee. Pastor Cosby and then Pastor Morgan had a new inspirational quote or sermon title for me. I posted them and cleaned the glass covering. I hung individual letters, which were organized in a wooden box.

Once in awhile I was fortunate enough to walk with Joan Elliott, the Episcopal pastor's daughter. I had a crush on her for a few months, and she tolerated me. I should have kept a couple of notes we exchanged at school. She's famous now.

Although I have many good memories of life and times at First Baptist Church, what stuck with me was the variety of pastors, traveling evangelists, missionaries, assorted other speakers and music groups that frequented our pulpit. I had a Bible with autographs of everyone who preached at our church. I started collecting signatures about fifth or sixth grade and by the time I left high school I had eighty-seven autographs. One day that Bible disappeared.

The evangelists came for week-long revivals. We had at least one thunderous revival a year there. Few members got revived, but over the years a few people got saved.

Christian college musical groups, usually choirs, came to our church to present quick concerts and some recruiting material. Most of those groups were pretty good. Missionaries usually came for Sunday night services and gave a slide presentation of their work in the country where they missioned. They asked for our prayers and money.

• • •

Verily, Verily I Say Unto You Department. You seen one missionary slide presentation, you seen 'em all.

• • •

One weekend early in my high school years, our church burned its mortgage. The church building and the parsonage next door were free and clear, thanks to the sacrificial offerings from 50 years of members. It was a time to celebrate. The mortgage paper was placed on a silver platter and set ablaze. In our church, no one applauded or clapped for anyone or anything. It just wasn't done. But I thought this little ceremony was a beautiful exception to the rule. But no, not in the First Baptist Church. Instead, we sang a joyful hymn and went out to Rogers' ranch, north of Douglas for a good, old-fashioned all-church barbecue. Ah, but it wasn't just any barbecue.

The cooking started Saturday. One cow, two hogs and two lambs were sacrificed for our celebration dinner. They all went into pits for twenty-four hours of cooking. We arrived at the picnic with a widow lady. The smell of that meat rushed into the car and I staggered straight to it. I grabbed a plate and got in line. Mr. Thompson asked me if I'd like some pork.

"Okay," I said. "Did you cook all this meat?" I asked.

"Well, I helped." He piled on several chunks of pork. "Some beef?"

"Sure," I said. He sawed off a big slab of beef and plunked it on my plate.

"How 'bout some lamb? Want some lamb?"

I never had lamb before. "I guess so," I said. My plate was loaded.

I was a little embarrassed with all that meat on my plate. Could I clean up my plate? Was my mother watching? I looked around. Everybody else had mounds of food and didn't seem embarrassed at all. I didn't have room for the other things.

There was a table with nothing but watermelon slices—and flies. Another table, one that my mom helped cover, was covered with cakes and pies and cookies and pudding—all home-made from scratch the day before. Salads, casseroles and vegetables were everywhere. Under one of the shady trees was a freezer loaded with several flavors of hand-cranked ice cream. There was home-made bread and melting butter. Twelve jars of Dad's honey. Home-made jams and jellies, pickles and relishes.

There are wonderful meals and there are wonderful meals. But for a really wonderful meal, you should have been there!

There were flies everywhere, too. Who cared? I sat down with the boys in my Sunday School class, shooed the flies off my plate and took a little bite of lamb. A bright, heavenly light shone round about me. I heard angels singing the "Hallelujah Chorus." I respectfully stood up and looked around for the Pearly Gates. I wasn't in heaven, but I think I was close. Just a little taste of lamb and every nerve in my body jerked alive. I sat down, took another bite and shivered in the sunshine. Never in my life had anything so wonderfully delicious entered my mouth.

"*Hallelujah!*" I heard again.

"Here, Kenyon," I said to Tom Kenyon. "You want this piece of beef?"

"Heck, yeah!"

"Anybody want this pork?" Somebody, maybe everybody, grabbed my pork. "It's a dead pig," I reminded them and returned to my lamb. I ate lamb. With a mouthful, I went back for still more lamb. Mr. Thompson sure knew how to help cook lamb! I told him so, even though it's not polite to talk with your mouth full. "I just helped," he repeated. I went back again and again. I noticed his daughter Margaret was waddling around like me, too, and made a mental note to take lamb eating lessons from her. All those other crazy people were wasting their time on cake and ice cream and watermelon and stuff. I decided that lamb is God's meat of choice. Surely you've heard of the lamb of God.

It required a good walk through a sandy desert gully to get myself somewhat back to normal. A bunch of us teenagers wandered around—even put pennies on the railroad tracks. A freight train came along and flattened them for us. But we were too full and the sun was too warm for anything more exciting.

About five o'clock, I caught a ride home with Karen Kenyon and her boyfriend. Margaret Richardson sat across the back seat from me, slathering on fresh makeup. She and Karen had some sort of a silly girl secret going between them. I was too full, too tired and too sleepy to pay much attention.

Suddenly Margaret said, "Come here, Paul." Before I even had a chance to move, she grabbed my head, pulled me to her and blotted her lipstick on my left cheek. Karen watched and giggled. Her boyfriend was grinning into his rearview mirror. All those senses that the lamb had awakened now joyfully fired up again. Margaret sat back and returned her makeup kit to her purse as if nothing ever happened.

"I didn't think you would do it," Karen snickered. Margaret smiled at me and winked.

"*Hallelujah!*"

I don't know what Margaret was thinking, but I was thinking she wasn't my sister anymore.

First Baptist Church had several nice weekends over the years—and week days, too. We were another family that gathered frequently at the corner of Tenth Street and E Avenue. There were about a hundred fifty of us. When I was little, the ladies of the church family met on a particular day of the week and gathered around a quilting frame. It was fascinating to watch the ladies quilt by hand. They were artists. Women who brought small children, like my mom, let them run unfettered around the church yard all morning. By the time I was a teenager, they stopped quilting. I don't know why, and I don't know where the quilts went.

When Pastor Morgan arrived as our new minister, the first thing he did was order up an extensive clean-up, spruce-up. The exposed beams were dusted and polished, the sanctuary walls were patched and repainted and a new air conditioning system was installed. Every church member chipped in one way or another. All the boys in my age bracket, and their dads, went down in the basement and dug a hole for the big, new A/C unit. It took us several nights, but one hot Sunday morning we walked into the coolest service in town. We sang praises that Sunday. Yes, we did! How *nice*!

Pot luck dinners were one of my favorite reasons for going to church. Pot lucks were frequent and delicious, and at those dinners in the fellowship room we grew to know, respect and love one another. And eat each other's casseroles and Jell-O salads.

Praises, potlucks, get-togethers, hole-diggings, fellowship just for the sake of fellowship, Easter egg hunts, tears of joy and tears of sorrow, Sunday School classes, prayer meetings and business meetings, weddings and funerals, celebrations and even missionary slide presentations drew us all together because we were an altogether lovely family who worshipped together in one of the loveliest buildings in Cochise County.

Once family, always family. We have scheduled a Bright Day when we all get together again to sing "Hallelujah" with those angels I heard out at Rogers' ranch.

"...*in Christ, we who are many form one body, and each member belongs to all the others.*"

—Romans 12:5

Miscellaneous Quirks

Designer Clothing. If you want to decorate a T-shirt, save up several pop bottle caps. A coffee can is a good place to keep them. Inside each cap is a flat piece of cork that seals the bottle. Remove the cork. Put the cap on the outside of the shirt, push the cork back into the cap from the inside of the shirt. Artistically arrange the caps, or see how many you can put on a shirt. Use an old T-shirt, because your mother will huff and puff if you ruin a good one. When you play war games, put the caps on the collar of your big brother's old shirt. That's a little harder, but you get to be the general.

The Old Prognosticator. Agua Prieta had a little radio station that, for awhile, broadcast programs in English, including two daily hours of American Rock 'n' Roll. On his way to work, the DJ stopped briefly at the port and asked my dad for a weather report. Dad almost always said, "Clear skies, sunny and hot." The DJ made a big deal of his weather report, which often was different than the official one. "I heard it from the Old Prognosticator," he said every time. Other than his family and the DJ, no one knew that Dad was the Old Prognosticator.

Wright's Grocery wasn't on Seventh Street. It was on the corner of A Avenue and Twenty-third Street in a stone building. That's where we bought most of our groceries while I was growing up. When Mr. Doug Wright retired, my folks then bought groceries at the new A.J. Bayless superstore out between Ninth Street and Tenth Street.

My mom sat on her couch and called in her order of groceries. Later that day, Mr. Wright's brother Paul delivered them. He parked his pickup in the Neatest Driveway on Earth and toted our groceries inside. He came in the house calling, "Groceries," wearing a long leather apron, and put everything on the kitchen table. It didn't matter how much was ordered; he brought in little orders or big orders. Paul had no bags. He brought everything in collapsible wooden milk crates. Occasionally, Ruth or I was given the chore to call in the order.

If we were not home, the back door was unlocked and Paul brought the groceries in anyway. If he had ice box items, he put them in there so they wouldn't spoil. It was a neat system; better than the Internet, because it was all done on handwritten credit chits.

Phelps-Dodge had a grocery store on Tenth and G. They had several men who delivered groceries to their customers, too. They did the same thing as Paul Wright, except they drove orange pickups.

Mrs. Wright, by the way, was my Third and Fourth Grades teacher.

Mayberry? Douglas had a friendly telephone operator who knew us by the sound of our voice. I didn't know her name then and I don't know it now.

"Number please," she asked when we lifted the receiver. (They all did).

"9-0-1-R."

"Is this Paul Nichols? How are you today?"

"Fine." Then she rang Doug Foster's number for me. Sometimes, Douglas was a lot like Mayberry. Our number was 6-1-2-J. Later it became EMpire 4-5804.

All the Douglas phones were on a party line. That is, two or three houses shared the same telephone line. It was possible to hear another person's telephone conversation just as if it were your own. Of course, if you picked up the receiver and heard someone talking, you put it back in a hurry. Or if you asked for a number and the operator said, "I'm sorry, that line is busy," she meant that someone on that party line was tying up two or three other phones, too. We were on a party line with the Verdugos behind us on Eighth Street. If we really, really needed the phone when another party was talking, it was okay to politely interrupt and explain that we needed the phone for an emergency.

What was an emergency? Well, if a stranger talked to your sister and offered her some candy; that would be one. If your big brother was running with scissors and poked his eye out, that counted, too. That's about it.

Stamps. Many times Dad mailed a package with a letter tucked inside. On the outside of the package, in bold letters, he wrote: "Letter

Enclosed." He not only paid the postage for the package, but bought an extra stamp for the letter inside.

I tried to convince him that he was paying postage on the entire contents of the package, regardless of what was inside. He didn't have to pay extra for the letter. He wouldn't hear of it. It was a letter and it needed postage. Oh well, a five-cent stamp didn't affect the budget that much.

Dad liked **baseball**. He encouraged me a lot, but I don't remember Neal or Noel ever having a whole lot to do with it. By the way, Little League came after their time. He played on a community softball team when he was a young man. However, he never understood the concept of a third of an inning. (Each out represents one third of an inning, no matter how many batters bat.) If five batters went up to the plate before the third out, then to him the inning was half done because half of the nine batters in the lineup had batted.

"Well, Mr. Nichols, when is it half over if only three batters go to the plate, and they all strike out?" Dad thought a couple of seconds, shook his head, and answered, "The kid can really pitch, can't he?"

Airplanes. Dad was afraid to fly. He dueled diamondback rattlers, but wouldn't get in anything that wasn't attached to the earth.

And other trips. Ruth and I entertained ourselves in the back of the car with comic books, Hardy Boys and Nancy Drew, a Big Chief Tablet to draw in, puzzle magazines and fussing. Ruth and her doll were required to stay on her side of the line. However, it was okay for me inch my way across the line onto her side any time I wanted.

We also scanned the desert highways looking for every letter of the alphabet—in order. The one who found them all first, on signs and such, won that game. We looked for different state license plates and claimed it as our own if we found it first. When we saw one of those new little Volkswagens, we yelled, "Slug bug!" Dad grouched at us if we innocently asked, "When are we going to get there?" There are more than two hundred telephone poles between Douglas and Elfrida.

Gum. Every Sunday morning about five minutes before we left for Sunday School, Dad went out and stood beside the car to smoke his pipe. When the rest of us got to the car he jammed his mouth full of three or four sticks of Wrigley's Doublemint chewing gum to kill his breath. Then off we went to Sunday School.

Mom's Iron. Almost every Sunday morning about a minute after we left for Sunday School, Mom gasped. "Oh, dear! Did I unplug the iron?" Dad circled the block, returned home and checked the unplugged iron. In all those years, she never forgot to unplug it. Not long ago I heard of a man who solved that problem by taking the iron to church.

"Watch your language, young man." Mom's hobby was correcting our English. "Dad took a picture of Ruth and I."

"...Ruth and *me*," she corrected.

"Ruth and me got our pictures taken," I corrected myself.

"Ruth and *I*..." she trumped.

[Sigh]

I'll say one thing: if Mom had been everybody's eighth grade English teacher, nobody would ever say "most importantly" or "secondly" or "lastly" or spell cooperation without a hyphen.

"Son, will you hook my bra for me?" It never bothered Mom to ask one of us boys to hook her bra.

"The Desert" was a three-block by six-block undeveloped area just three quick blocks up the street from 1122. It was a great place for building forts and playing war games. Usually a group of us went up there together, not just one or two boys. One time John Matson and Luis Rodriquez sneaked into our unprotected fort and peed into our canteens. Two or three guys drank from them before those two scalawags started hoo-hawing about it. "The Desert" is now a nice, large city park.

Tea Cups. About the time I was eight, Mom started a tea cup collection. Pretty soon, relatives and friends had an easy time of gift selection for her. I gave her quite a few cups, which I always bought at Posten's Hardware Store. Regardless of the occasion, Mom always counted on at least one beautiful tea cup. She kept most of them displayed on top of our buffet. Eventually, Dad asked a Mexican man to make a double set of display shelves for her. Dad mounted them on the wall, and the cups were the pride of the neighborhood. Mom proudly served tea or coffee to her guests, who always made a polite fuss over her display. They'd better. It was an impressive collection.

She had one attractive cup that stood on four little legs. It had an Oriental design on it, including a tiny, hand-laid gold chain. Oops. One day I snapped a leg off the cup. It was an accident. Honest. I was eleven or twelve, I'd say. I glued the leg back in place and put that cup on the back row of the buffet display.

A few years later, I heard Mom washing the cups, preparing for a group of church ladies. "What…? What?…*What happened here?*" she screamed. I hurried to the kitchen to see what was wrong.

"This cup has been broken and glued back together," she screamed again. "What happened to this cup?"

"I did that, Mom," I confessed. "It was an accident. You can hardly see the line where I fixed it," I pointed out. "I tried to do a good job."

"When did this happen?"

"About three years ago, I guess."

She squeezed it so hard it nearly squirted out of her soapy hands. She said nothing else, because she had used it several times without ever noticing the repair work. I don't know if the statute of limitations had run out on broken cup crimes or if she was so impressed with my excellent repair that she was speechless. I didn't hang around to find out.

Mom was smart. For every cup in her collection, she placed a piece of white, cloth bandage tape on the bottom and wrote a name it. Toward the end of her life she started distributing those cups to the people whose names were on the tapes. Most of them are now somewhere among her children and grandchildren's families. Marcie and my niece Debbie each have a section of the display shelves.

P.F. Flyers. I'm a slow runner. Anytime we kids had foot races, I either got beat or said "Forget it." My batting average would have been much higher if I had run from the batter's box to first base a little faster. When I ran, my feet felt like anvils. I smacked a triple once. When I finally clunked all the way to third base I was ready for retirement. Some oxygen would have been a nice treat about then.

We had no choice of brand names. We bought P.F. Flyers tennis shoes at Levy's Department Store, Phelps-Dodge Mercantile or Fair's

Sport Shop. Black, high-top, lace-up shoes with thick soles, *guaranteed* to help you run faster and jump higher. See? Right there in that comic book's inside cover is an ad promising I can run faster and jump higher.

There is something special about a new pair of tennis shoes. Tennies. It was almost ritualistic to put on a new pair of Flyers. Oh, no, I never wore them out of the store. When I got home, I put them on and laced them up, careful not to twist the laces. Then outside, with visions of flashing down Seventh Street, I clunked along as hard as always. Funny, I didn't run any faster. I jumped several times, but not any higher than the times before. Why couldn't I run faster and jump higher like the ads said?

We wore our Flyers till our toes wore holes in them. By that time, the soles were worn smooth, the canvas was filled with desert dust and the laces were black with dirt. Laces usually had a knot or two in them. We didn't buy new laces. We just knotted the old ones right on the spot.

When it was time to throw them away, I cut out the tongue for a dandy slingshot pouch. If Dad got to an old pair before I did, he set it aside until he went to the city dump. He put the shoes among the trash in an easy place for the Mexican boys to find.

Speaking of shoes, one of the most common living room display items was Baby's First Pair of Shoes. The shoes were dipped in liquid bronze and arranged on a polished chunk of wood, thus immortalizing them. They made good book ends, too. It seems like every home I entered had Baby's First Shoes on display somewhere. But not at our house.

"Gentlemen. Start... Your... *Engines!*" The Indianapolis 500 Mile Race always ran on Memorial Day. Didn't matter what day of the week; it was raced on Memorial Day. In fact, it was often referred to as the "Memorial Day" race. How that race became so special to me, I don't know, but I listened to the whole race every Memorial Day. When all the drivers and positions were listed in the *Arizona Republic*, I concocted a chart and followed the race on our radio.

Tony Hulman started the race about nine in the morning, Arizona time. It ended late in the afternoon. Sid Collins kept us up to the minute on the radio. After every ten laps, he gave us driver positions, which I quickly marked on my chart. And just before every commercial he said, "Stay tuned for The Greatest Spectacle in Racing." I listened to that race for about twelve years till my first year in the army.

"I wonder if they'll ever go as fast as a hundred and fifty miles an hour?"

"I doubt it. That's awful fast. But who knows? Maybe."

My favorite race was in 1958 when Jimmy Bryan won. He was a Phoenix man, so everybody in the state rooted for him for more than a few years. All of Arizona was happy and proud that day. Another good Indy driver, Bill Cheeseborough from Tucson, came to DHS when I was a senior and gave a talk about safe driving.

It's amazing how easy it is to clean the whole bathroom and how many dishes you can wash while the Indy 500 has your undivided attention.

Running Boards. Dad let us ride in the back of the pickup all we wanted. No standing up in the back or sitting on the side rails. But for short jaunts, such as from one group of beehives to another, we just hopped onto the running board.

For a few years, one of my favorite things was waiting at the corner for Dad to come home from work.

At four in the afternoon, I took up my station on the corner and peered down A Avenue. He came into view about Fourth Street. What a long wait those three blocks were. But he soon arrived and stopped at the corner. I stood on the running board and got to ride all the way into the Neatest Driveway on Earth—about fifty feet. Every ride was a grand ride. Sometimes, out of Dad's line of vision, I held on with only one hand. Don't tell him.

Horses. We didn't have any horses. Too expensive to maintain, I think. The Fosters had two horses almost all the time we lived at 1122. They were boarded in a small pen and shed out behind the YMCA, just beyond the railroad tracks. On summer mornings, if there was no neighborhood horseplay scheduled, Doug and I finished our paper routes, then rode our scooters out to get the horses. We rode them bareback to his house where the saddles were kept. Then it was off for a morning of sunburn somewhere out in the desert. Doug burned easily. I don't remember Ruth ever riding horses, but I suppose she did.

Snuff and Cookies. Mom had two elderly lady friends, Mrs. Still and Grandma Rice, who lived in a tiny home across from the junior high school. When Mom went to see them, Ruth and I went along, too. They always crocheted and knitted. Mrs. Still took me to the Phelps-Dodge Mercantile store once and bought me two Golden Books.

Grandma Rice dipped snuff. She sat in her wooden rocker needling away. Every so often, she stopped long enough to lean over the arm of her chair and spit snuff juice into a Hills Bros. coffee can.

Ruth and I never minded tagging along to Mrs. Littell's, another elderly widow. She lived on the corner of Fourteenth and D Avenue in a house that smelled like old wood and old body powder. We didn't mind going because the first order of business was cookies. She always offered us her homemade cookies, which were not small cookies, either. *Mmmm* Sometimes she encouraged us to take two.

Old Mrs. Littell became sick and fell into a deep and lengthy coma. Her heart beat gently, but the other ninety-nine percent of her body didn't work at all. It just lay on her bed at home. That was a disturbing time for my mom and the people at church. It was a time of heavy prayer. When Mrs. Littell's heart finally stopped, nobody cried. Mom showed a lot of compassion the day Mrs. Littell died. "I'm just so relieved," she said reverently.

Honey, Honey, Honey. Dad put his clear, golden honey on everything. Eggs, tomatoes, biscuits, coffee, ice cream, tea, fruit, bread, pancakes, sweet potatoes, hot or cold cereal of every kind, peanut butter sandwiches. He dipped carrots, celery sticks and green onions into the jar. He stuck his finger into the jar. If honey dripped somewhere unusual, like meat or spinach, it didn't bother him. He taught us how to blend butter and honey and call it Honeyscotch. He also taught us to eat our green peas off a knife. First stick the knife into the honey jar, then touch it to the peas. Lick the peas off the knife and do it again from the other side. However, if your mother is there, too—uh, not a good idea.

Corn on the Cob. How old was I that night? Ten? Eight? Twelve? That evening, we gnawed away at our corn on the cob like little mice at a garbage festival. Suddenly Dad said to whoever was listening, "I'll give you ten dollars if you can show me an ear of corn with an odd number of rows." He started gnawing again.

My sister and I gawked at each other—*Ten dollars!*—and started counting our rows. Who'd get the money first?

Even numbered. Even numbered. Even numbered. We grew corn in Our Back Yard so in the summer there was plenty of it. We had corn on the cob three and four nights a week. Even numbered, every one. Even numbered, every one.

Eventually, a handful of years passed and I was busy counting the corn rows one evening. Dad asked, "What are you doing?"

"Well, counting the rows."

"What for?"

What for? Had he forgotten?

"Cuz you said you'd give me ten dollars if I found one with odd rows."

"When did I tell you that?"

"A long time ago."

"I remember," said Ruth.

"Well, you're not going to find one. There aren't any, Son. There's never been any. There's never going to be any. All corn cobs have an even number of rows. Now just forget it."

Oh.

"I remember the days of long ago; I meditate on all your works and consider what your hands have done."

—Psalm 143:5

We Were Not Poor

When I was an adult, Mom told me that one year Dad's total income was $2,800. That was in the '50s. But what was money? We ate well, shared well, slept well, worked well and played well.

Is life genetic? Would I have wanted to give away my baseball glove if I hadn't seen Dad give away chickens and honey and firewood and fifty-cent pieces and my old tennies? Would I understand the miracle of tithing if Mom hadn't suggested that I tithe a paltry six dollars to Eunice? Would Marcie and Amy be as sweet as they are without all that honey running through my veins? Would Michael have flown to such heights if I hadn't stood on top of the world from the top of my tree house? What mistake would I have made if the First Baptist Church hadn't taught me to look for a Christian bride?

More than anything, we Nichols kids had a spiritual upbringing. And if our parents didn't teach us, there were plenty of folks at the First Baptist Church who did. Eunice Peevey got in her two cents worth—and it was mighty valuable, too. People at First Baptist revered my parents and polished all of us kids like precious little jewels. Betina and Blanca always asked the blessing over lunch—*en Español*. Even though I hardly understood a word of them, those were rich and beautiful prayers.

Our neighborhood was plump with playgrounds right at our fingertips. Our own yards were good starters. We had two baseball fields up at Clawson School and a football field, to boot. Just up the street was "The Desert." We had street playgrounds, which we generously shared with traffic. The vacant lots were the next best thing to the Holy Land.

Doug Foster's back yard was a pretty little park. His yard had two big plum trees and a cherry tree between them. The Fosters had a full, rich grape arbor out by the alley and they kept a garden, too. Good munchies all summer long. There was plenty of grass for wrestling, boxing, football. The steps at his back door were usually shaded. They made a nice place to sit and shoot BB guns.

And we had family. Lucky me: I got to have two older brothers and a little sister. Dad told stories. But he never wrote them down for us. "Naw, that's just the way we lived back then," he excused. He told us things he'd done, places he'd been and people he'd seen. While he was at it, he tried to pull our legs. Not having Dad's life stories in my hands is what prompted me to open up this treasure chest full of my own memories.

When we lived at 1122 Seventh Street, Neal, Noel and I went to trade school at COBY (College of Our Back Yard). Dad was the Dean of Boys. We became carpenters, mechanics, brick masons, painters, beekeepers, electricians… It's the only school I know of that doesn't charge anything. So I guess life is genetic. You should see the junk I keep now just because it might come in handy someday.

• • •

Oh, wait! Department. There's a free driving school out at Buster's, too.

• • •

We had friends. Friends that held us all by the heartstrings; held us close and held us up. The Richardsons were so close to us that we walked into each other's homes without knocking. Doug Foster was my best friend. Seventh Street moms never let a-one of us get away with anything. They loved us too much to let us get ourselves into trouble. They hollered at us in Spanish and English. Even if we didn't understand, we understood.

My dad had friends that lived far into Mexico. One Mexican family lived much closer to El Paso than Douglas, but they chose to drive across the dusty Sonora Desert to Agua Prieta for a few minutes with Dad at the port. I had a few stinky friends out at the city dump who showed me that we were not poor. I never knew him, but John Slaughter helped drill my roots. He was a friend, just as much as those Apaches who drank from the same Artesian water spring as I did. *Imagine!* I literally drank Cochise County history.

No one had as many friends as we did, and most of them lived in Our Back Yard beehives.

Laugh if you want, but a radio hour of schmaltzy accordion music on "The Lawrence Welk Show" was how I learned that music makes your soul swoon. (You know why they invented bassoons? Because they make good kindling for an accordion fire.) The Gadsden Hotel and "Heartbreak Hotel" are cousins in my heart. Bill Haley and The Comets, Jerry Lee Lewis, Elvis Presley, Chuck Berry, Fabian and Buddy Holly were nighttime friends who visited via my little white plastic radio. Without them, I wouldn't know how to do the Twist. I can listen to good music twenty-four hours a day. I have to confess: those bitter piano lessons and two years in the DHS A Cappella choir taught me a lot about music. So did a few hot afternoons when I cranked my Victrola out at Buster's.

Oh sure, I always wanted an electric train for Christmas, but I always got socks. However, if you don't get something for Christmas, you get to keep dreaming for it.

• • •

Update Department: My little sister and my big brother gave me my first electric train at Christmas 2007. Dreams do come true.

• • •

What if I hadn't fallen out of the chinaberry tree and loosened Mom's neck? I'll bet that saved Dad a ton of money.

I had free legal counsel most of the time I was growing up. When it was time for a whipping, my little sister came to my defense—screaming for mercy.

I take great delight in children because Debbie, Cozette and Valerie freely delighted us every day.

What's the value of the tinkering, whistling sound of sunrise? That's easy: the same value as the slurping sound of a Dairy Queen ride. Saturday Afternoon Matinees were a dime well-invested. We didn't pay anything for fifteen minutes of my dad's tall tales.

We were well-educated, too. Dad taught us about the stars—the ones that were just a little bit beyond our fingertips but high over the Arizona nighttime desert. He taught us about birds and bees—real ones. We used back issues of the *National Geographic* to travel the world and *Arizona Highways* to travel the state. We learned the fine points of base-stealing up at Clawson School. Thanks to Grandmother I learned to tell stories. Thanks to Grandmother's son, I learned to tell tall tales. Thanks to Grandmother, I learned to write Thank You notes. Get it? I learned to write.

Our folks were somewhat stern and rigid, but they weren't afraid to spoil us. Anytime we wanted, they let us gobble a handful of raisins. I never liked raisins much so I unzipped a banana. They let us stick our fingers straight into the honey jar, lick 'em and stick 'em in again. Dad let us pour too much honey on Mom's delicious hot biscuits. Mom let us lick beaters, which are ten times sweeter if your brothers and sister aren't home to share.

When I was just a tiny thing, I was allergic to cow's milk. The only alternative was goat's milk. It's rancid. I probably never had more than two swallows of the sickening stuff. (I think goat cheese with herbs is pretty tasty, though.) Praise the Lord, somehow I overcame the milk allergy by the time I was five and got to have all the cow's milk I wanted. I especially liked the kind that came in a cone or in a quart container from the Dairy Queen.

Mom didn't scold us much when she caught us drinking milk straight from the carton. I think she was happy we were able to drink it at all. She made sure that ice cream was carefully and equally divided: 4/5 for Dad, 1/5 for the rest of us.

I don't know how much it cost to live in a home flowing with milk and honey, but it must be a lot, because we were not poor.

*"When God gives a man wealth and possessions, and enables him to enjoy them, to accept his lot and be happy in his work—
this is a gift of God."*

—Ecclesiastes 5:19

What Do You Want to be
When You Grow Up?

I distinctly remember answering the question: *What do you want to be when you grow up?*

A bunch of folks were out in front of the church after service. It was hot. I wore a thin sport shirt and pink denim pants, which were in at the time. I was six years old and climbing on the wrought iron fence.

I answered, "I want to be a dad."

My dream came true. I got to be Dad to the greatest kids I ever knew.

"I have no greater joy than to hear that my children are walking in the truth."

—3 John 1:4

Half the Fun of Christmas

We opened gifts on Christmas Eve because Mom spent Christmas morning preparing world class Christmas dinners. Only once do I remember opening on Christmas morning and that was because Dad worked the swing shift the night before.

We always bought our Christmas trees, because there are no Christmas tree farms in the desert. We went down to a vacant lot on G Avenue and picked one out. While Dad was setting it up, Neal or Noel went out to the shed and dragged in a wide box of ornaments. Ruth and I added popcorn chains and colorful paper chains that we made at school. The tree wasn't officially decorated until we put the angel on top. Noel was always the one who got to do that.

At school, all the students decorated the walls and windows with paper snowflakes and other typical childhood Christmas art. We always had two full weeks of Christmas vacation from school. At church, on the Sunday evening before Christmas, all the children sang in the Christmas pageant. All the little boys put on their father's bath robes and called themselves shepherds and wise men. All the little girls wrapped themselves in old bed sheets and called themselves angels. Whoever had the biggest doll donated it so the cardboard box manger could have a Baby Jesus. Afterward, all the kids got a long net stocking with candy and an orange. There was always an orange at the bottom. The first year those stockings were distributed I was seven or eight years old. I was surprised to see them and politely said, "No, thank you" when one was offered to me. I declined because I wasn't sure if Dad would pay for it. But when I saw the other kids—including Ruth—getting a free stocking full of candy I changed my mind.

Back home, we looked forward to parcel post packages. Traditionally, Aunt Crosie always sent a box of homemade divinity with walnuts and little bags of her glass candy. She always included a couple of towels that she had stencil-painted. Some years she included pink and green popcorn balls, which she also made.

Grandmother sent a package of exciting things like colorful argyle socks.

Half the fun of Christmas is shaking a present to figure out what it is. The other half is counting how many presents you have under the tree—and your little sister better not have more than you!

Another half is laying on the floor close to the tree and watching the lights twinkle. We had strings of bubble lights that intrigued me to no end. On a cold December evening, I dreamt under those lights all night long.

Speaking of dreaming on the floor, half the fun of Christmas is flopping on the floor with the Sears and Roebuck and Montgomery Ward winter catalogs and drooling over page after page of Christmas toys. Sometimes Ruth and I both lay there, propped up on our elbows, telling each other how much we wanted that and that and that and, well, everything on the page. She always loitered over the dolls and strollers, make-up kits and authentic ballerina costumes. I wanted to hurry on to the fire trucks and electric trains and toy soldiers. I dreamed for an electric train more than anything else.

The best half of Christmas is being sent into the back bedroom with Ruth to anxiously wait for Noel to ring the doorbell and holler, "Ho. Ho. Ho."

"Well, who is this?" Mom feigned every Christmas Eve at seven o'clock. "Paul! And Ruth! Come quickly! Look who's here!" No matter how fast we ran to the living room, there was never anyone there. Just Mom, Dad, Neal and Noel. We never looked for anyone, anyway. We headed straight for the tree. "Oh, you just missed him," Noel always teased with a grin. Ruth and I were never taught about Santa Claus. We learned about him from pictures and rumors at school. (My brother Neal once confessed, "...when I still believed in Santa.")

The Nichols were not well-to-do folks. The kids usually got a special toy or game for Christmas and several things we "needed"— shirts and belts and underwear and still more socks.

Dad always got a shirt and a tie and a new Crescent wrench. Mom always got towels and aprons. Dad was usually romantic enough to give her something modern with an electrical cord dangling from it. Her first electric toaster was a fantastic addition to our kitchen. That

Christmas Eve we must have toasted two loaves of bread. Two slices of bread toasted evenly on both sides at the same time. "Oh, wow!"

One year, Ruth received a portable pink record player for her 45 rpm records. It closed up like a suitcase and she carried it anywhere she wanted. That made for easy gift giving for me. I gave her a rock 'n' roll record a couple of years. The ones on the Top Ten chart cost a dollar, the others only eighty-five cents. She didn't get the ones in the Top Ten.

There were four Christmases when I got cheated out of a present. I was thirteen when my California cousin Ruth Ann sent me a bottle of Old Spice after shave lotion. Well, her parents did. "What am I supposed to do with this?" I wondered. "I'll just give it to Dad, I guess."

When I was fourteen the same thing happened. "Again?"

When I was fifteen the same thing...

When I was sixteen...

When your mom tells you to send a thank you note, don't blather on about your gift. You might get another one just like it. I have no idea what my folks picked out for Ruth Ann on my behalf, but I'll bet it wasn't four consecutive bottles of something she'd never use.

One year just before Christmas, I happened upon a dirty pop bottle that was almost fully buried in a vacant lot. Hmmm. I wrapped the dirty bottle in some meat wrapping paper that Mom was about to toss out. With a green crayon I wrote, "To Noel from Paul." Ha. Ha.

"Hey, Thanks, Paul," he said. "I can get the nickel deposit for this!" Later on Mom scolded me.

One bittersweet Christmas, I was ripping and tearing through an unusually large number of gifts when I noticed Neal sitting on the couch just watching everyone. He was home from college and had already opened his gift. A belt, I think. Just one present? That's not fair. I looked around to see if I had something to give him. Nothing, really. I went back to my presents, but I lost my enthusiasm.

Now I must tell you that there is no such thing as a White Christmas. That's as much of a myth as Santa Claus. Oh, no. In Douglas, Christmas is a bright, sunny day, the temperature about 65 degrees, and all the kids outside in light jackets. Santa will melt in that red, hot suit he wears.

Half the fun of Christmas is drifting outside into the warm sunshine to find out what your friends got. Here and there was a new bike and a couple of footballs, and naturally, new dolls. Everybody got some kind of clothes, but we didn't waste our time telling about those things. We wanted to know about the good stuff like cap pistols with holsters, Red Ryder BB guns and chemistry sets. By nine o'clock, all the kids in the neighborhood knew what each other had received.

Except for the big dinner, Christmas was pretty much over.

Other than Lavonda and her girls when they lived next door, I don't think we had any relatives in our home during the Christmas season. We might have, though, because we had some Christmas dinners that included more people than the Nichols. Mom fixed the whole thing herself. Just before we ate, Dad read from Luke, Chapter 2, the pretty story of Jesus' birth.

The Nichols were not well-to-do folks. When I was a junior in high school, my parents gave me a gift that came in a small, square box. Not the kind where I'd find another pair of socks. Besides, I'd already opened that box. I always opened the socks first, saving the best for last.

"Hmmm? This is different. Wonder what it is?"

I was sitting on the floor. Just my luck: the box was difficult to unwrap and just as difficult to open. I picked at the stubborn tape and frantically riffled through my imagination. "What on earth?"

I finally broke open the box. I looked in, but still couldn't figure out what it was. It was bright and shiny and upside-down. I never had a bright, shiny, upside-down gift before.

"*A watch!*" My eyes saw it, but my brain didn't. "*No! It can't be!*"

"We can't… They don't… Where did…? How could they afford this?" I never had a watch before. With uncontained disbelief I broke into shaking and sobbing—right in front of my sister.

"Well, Paul, what's wrong, honey?" Mom asked with a proud smile. I just shook my head and kept on sobbing. I never dreamt that my parents would sacrifice so much money on me. It took me a week to take that nine dollar Timex watch out of the box, wind it up and wear it.

Half the fun of Christmas was discovering that the Nichols were more well-to-do than I thought.

"No eye has seen, no ear has heard, no mind has conceived what God has prepared for those who love him."

—1 Corinthians 2:9

The Last Day at 1122 Seventh Street

It was moving time. Wintertime. Joe Pinedo gave me a ride home from school. I was expecting to do my fair share of packing and moving—but when I went in the house it was empty. You know, empty; nothing in it. Hollow; every step echoed. Nobody was home. Nobody was ever coming home again.

Our Back Yard—the home for beehives, bent nails, burn barrels, chickens, clothes lines, deep holes, fences, frontier forts, gardens and grape vines; kids from everywhere; overnight campouts, second-hand lumber, slingshot battles, tomato plants, tinkering tools, tree houses—was barren.

The apricot tree had been cut down and hauled off, my tree house with it.

The shed row had been ruthlessly cleaned out, except for the persistent smell of worn out mothballs and oil-stained shelves. All those magazines were smoldering in the city dump. And maybe the man on the bulldozer was reading a few.

The Neatest Driveway on Earth was raked bare of its treasures and lay there like a lonely lane to nowhere. The garage was empty, filled with sour dust. It had a severe, sad sag I never noticed before.

My adventures at 1122 Seventh Street were over. There was nothing there anymore, so I left my heart behind the honeysuckle trellis and slipped out the back gate. I cut through the alley and walked four blocks up to our new place. We no longer lived just seven blocks from the Mexican border.

"He makes all things beautiful in its time."

—Ecclesiastes 3:11

One Last Soft Touch

Not many months before Mom passed away up in Kansas, she and I sat on the edge of her bed with a box of old photos. She came across a picture of Blanca. She wistfully paused and softly brushed her fingertips across it, touching the time that Blanca and Betina graced our home. Then she humbly asked, "What were we thinking to keep you kids from dating Mexican girls?" She paused another minute. "Are they Mexican now, or are they Chicano?"

"They're called Hispanic now," I said softly, "but I still prefer Mexican."

"Those Mexican girls I worked with—Hispanic? That's pretty.— why, they're some of the sweetest, Christian young women I ever met. And Blanca…and Betina…" A teardrop fell into her quiet moment.

"Whatever possessed us, honey?"

"The memory of the righteous will be a blessing…"

—Proverbs 10:7

Friend of the Bees, Part 3

Dad died in his bedroom when I was almost 38 years old. I lived in Vancouver, Washington at the time. Mike, Marcie and Amy were well on their way to becoming fine Christian young people.

The coroner said dad suffered a heart attack, but that ain't necessarily so. You see, he loved his children, his church, his bees and his pickup. A little bit like Job of the Old Testament, Dad lost a son, his bees and his pickup all in one week. Not only that, but younger, stronger men had taken his place at church.

Suddenly, in January 1981, my brother Noel died in Enterprise, Alabama. Too frail to travel there, my parents stayed home. With family approval, I went to their house instead of Noel's funeral.

The day I arrived back in Douglas, Dad had just sold the last of his bees and equipment. A day or two later he sold his pickup. He and I sadly watched the new owner drive it away. Dad lost his son. Dad lost his bees. Dad lost his pickup. All this grief was apparently more than he could bear in one fell swoop. And so, on February 3, 1981, only ten days after Noel died, he sat down on the edge of his bed and—just like that—died of a broken heart. He was seventy-six and he didn't suffer.

Loving, long-time friends filled the mortuary funeral chapel. Many Arizona and Mexico communities were represented—from all over the country, actually. Pat and Lloyd came from Kansas. Lavonda set aside her own grief and flew to Douglas. I flew back from Washington State. Neal and Beverly came from Kansas. Ruth from Chicago. People I didn't know came from all over the place. Beekeepers, government officials, *Oficiales Mexicanos*. From Douglas came most of the church members, of course. The local college sent folks; the whole camera club was there. Friends of each of us kids showed up. From Agua Prieta came folks from the churches Dad helped and loved, shopkeepers, his barber, poor people who walked to the mortuary... The list goes on and on.

And Mom? Mom was a wonder! From the moment she knew, she greeted everyone graciously and accepted their condolences with dignity. She was a tower of strength—a really short one.

Mr. Page, the funeral director, told me that Dad's was the most attended funeral in the history of Douglas. The eulogy was full of hope and the promise that Dad was in heaven waiting for us.

It was all nice, but his funeral felt incomplete for me. Something was left out. Even back at Mom's house with all her friends stopping by, I felt like Dad's funeral was unfinished. Something was missing.

That night, a bunch of family sat around the living room eating spicy tamales and telling tall tales. We had a good time. We laughed. We had fun. My brother Neal, the new patriarch of the Nichols family, proudly pointed out, "Nothing would please Dad any more than what we're doing right now." He was right.

The next morning—a bright, sunny, cool, birthday for me—I went to Calvary Cemetery on Third Street. I deliberately went alone to try and shake that uncomfortable feeling. From the car, I looked at Dad's grave, tenderly and respectfully piled high with funeral flowers. I sat in the car and just gazed for a minute; the window rolled up against the windy February chill. Under those flowers lay my dad in the desert we all loved so much.

When I opened the car door I heard them. I didn't quite see them, but I heard them. And I smiled. Bees! Bees, bees, bees! Of course! The bees! Hundreds of dancing bees were sipping sweet nectar from Dad's flowers. Their muzzic—*oh, what sweet muzzic!*—is what I heard. I hurried in among them while they cheerfully zzipped among the flowers. "Wow! Hi," I said. I stood among them for ten or fifteen minutes, smiling the whole time. I knelt down and picked up a long stem of gladiolas and watched several bees scurry all over it. I gingerly returned it. I stayed there and prayed a little. Occasionally a bee or two wandered around on my jacket—two or three kissed my cheeks—but soon zzoomed back to their delicious flowers. I was completely alone among a thousand friends who seemed just as happy to see me. Here we were, hanging out at Dad's gravesite, just three blocks from the Mexican border. What a birthday!

The bees knew who I was and they knew exactly what I needed. They came to honor my father. Their visit made his passing complete for me. Dad was in good handzz. I finally told them, "I gotta go now. See you later." This moment was something I had to share with Mom. A few bees escorted me back to the car and I drove away filled with a peace that passes all understanding.

But wait! Picture this. Suppose all those friendly bees had attended his burial the day before. Imagine the frenzzy! When, where and how fast would the pallbearers drop the coffin? How quick would mourners mourn? Would the preacher ever get to pray? Would there be solemn words? How many directions would everyone run? Would friendly, well-meaning bees try to herd us back to the casket? Would Dad ever get buried? Would the Lord calmly turn to him and say, "Look at them down there. What a hoot."?

Now there's a story I wish I could tell.

"How precious in the eyes of the Lord is the death of his saints."

—Psalm 116:15

What Ever Happened to...?

The last time I saw **Doug Foster** he came to offer condolences to my parents the week that Noel died. Then he himself died far too young (age thirty-nine): about a year, year and a half after Dad died. He's still my best friend. I got to visit with **Mike Foster** for a couple of hours in 2008. I saw his mom **Eleanor**, too, and got all teary-eyed when we hugged. **Jimmy** lives in Phoenix. If you look closely, you might see him "working the chains" for the Arizona Cardinals and Arizona State University Sun Devils football games. Doug's sister **Donna** and I exchange e-mail occasionally—and we got to have coffee together in 2009. I'm still blessed to have grown up with the Fosters.

Joe Pinedo's voice broke; he had to leave the opera. His stage is a computer now and he lives in Texas.

Joe Tippy died far too young.

Joan Elliott is Joan Elliott Pickart. You can find her romance novels in your local library and bookstores. She wrote more than eighty. She still lives in Arizona. When she was over fifty, she adopted a Chinese baby. Bless her heart.

Beverly Morgan surprised me with a telephone call after I finished the text of this book. So now I *do* know where she went. She married a sailor and went all over the world with him. After he passed away, Beverly settled in Florida and now works at a college.

Betty Hooper, Luis Rodriguez, Rene Friend and **Gloria Amaya**. I don't know what happened to them. I'd like to.

Edmond Lewis does something in the Las Vegas school district.

Les Stimac lives in Phoenix, then California, then Phoenix, then California, then Phoenix... His wife Pat died several years ago and he married a long-time friend, Anita. We touch bases every two years or so, and it's like no time has passed at all. We saw each other in 2008. He's like a brother.

Coach Ike Sharp was inducted into the Arizona Baseball Coaches Hall of Fame in June 2005. God bless him.

Betina and **Blanca** live in my heart alongside Noel, my parents and **Eunice Peevey.**

Hollis Phillips. One afternoon, in the Spring of '65, possibly '66, I went to watch Hollis pitch against the Arizona State University Sun Devils. I was even able to lean over the bullpen rail and exchange a couple of "Hey, how ya' doin?"'s with him. Then I watched Reggie Jackson, Sal Bando, and Rick Monday pound the living daylights out of him. Those three batters alone sent him to a first inning shower. It was sad to see my friend go lugging off the field and out of sight. I haven't seen Hollis since, but I happen to know that the rest of his life was much less brutal.

Buster's Victrola. *Grrrrrrrr!!*

Willard Henry. Immediately after his widowed mother died in 1958 or so, he disappeared into a state-run home up in Phoenix.

Tom and Margaret Richardson. I saw June and Margaret at my mother's funeral in 1988. Ruth and I even had a short meal with them afterward, but we all departed into the night wind. However, thanks to my sister-in-law Beverly, Margaret and I have reconnected. Margaret's now the prettiest girl in Texas, podner. Well, right after Darby and Amy.

My sister **Ruth** has lived in Chicago since 1968. Right after Christmas 2008, she married Arnie Felske. Their grandchildren "gave them away" in a deliciously fun wedding. God smiles and blesses.

My brother **Noel** passed away ten days before Dad. He served twenty years in the US Army and a few years for the State of Alabama. He never got to see his grandkids.

Debbie lives in Texas; **Cozette** and **Valerie** live in Alabama and Tennessee with active families. **Lavonda** remarried and claims she was blessed to have the country's two greatest husbands. Probably so.

Neal and Beverly have lived in the same Kansas house for over thirty years. Their four kids and several grandkids are scattered from there to the west coast.

Ruth and Paul in front; Neal and Noel behind us. I doubt if more than three photos were ever taken of us four kids together. Dad took this photo in '50 or '51. Courtesy of my sister Ruth.

The First Baptist Church is still beautiful.

The Smelter in Douglas and the Copper Queen Mine in Bisbee were shut down several years ago for ecological reasons. The air in Sulphur Springs Valley is now clean and pure. That's what the brochure says, anyway.

D Hill is still there, of course, but doesn't get the tender loving care and special treatment it deserves.

Slaughter's Ranch is a tourist attraction.

Agua Prieta is now ten times bigger than Douglas.

1122 Seventh Street. The cedar trees in the front yard have been replaced. The chinaberry tree I fell from is gone, and so is the fence I fell onto. The garage is gone, too. I doubt if there are any beehives in the back yard. The honeysuckle trellis is missing.

1122 Seventh Street (2008), featuring The Neatest Driveway on Earth. The building in the back (L) is the shed where Neal, Noel and I had our bedroom; where Mom stored her stuff and where Dad kept his tools. A tall, thick honeysuckle trellis used to shade this side of the house. The cooler cools the house from the west side now. Or did. 1122 Seventh Street is boarded up and abandoned.

". . .so the next generation would know them, even the children yet to be born, and they in turn would tell their children."

—Psalm 78:6

Epilogue: The Star of the Show

October 2008

Douglas High School sponsored an all-alumni reunion in October 2008 to celebrate the 100th anniversary of our school's first graduating class. Gloria and I attended. Among many friends from years gone by we enjoyed a weekend of Cochise County, Douglas, G Avenue, Douglas High School, Agua Prieta and the First Baptist Church. I regret that this was the first reunion I attended. What was I thinking to ignore all the other ones? It was a wonderful and unforgettable weekend.

When we drove away from Douglas to return home, past the blank space where the smelter used to be, Gloria said to me, "Your dad was the star of the show."

"Huh?"

We were there Friday, Saturday and Sunday morning. In that time, person after person said, "I remember your Dad..." They didn't say that they remembered my mom or anyone else in the family, just "I remember your Dad..." Then a story followed. These are only a few of the remarks they shared. I needed a recorder.

"Your dad...

- ...was always kind to me. He always said something nice whenever I went through the Port."

- ...just tapped on my car door a few times and let me pass through without any questions."

- ...told me to go home and say 'hi' to my folks and then go straight to bed" [after some under-aged drinking in Agua Prieta].

- ...asked if he should call my parents to let them know I was on the way home?" [after some under-aged drinking in Agua Prieta].

- ...was my camera buddy..."

256

- ...asked me, 'Do I need to inspect the trunk of your car?' and I always said, 'No, Mr. Nichols.' [even though there were several bottles of hooch back there]. But he knew."

- ...his honey was the best I ever ate. I still remember it."

- "I named my son after your Dad—Christopher Paul. Whenever I went through the Port, Mr. Nichols always said, 'If it's a boy, name him after me.' So we did. And I'm glad we did. Mr. Nichols was always real nice to us. We really liked him."

"Let your light shine before men in such a way that they may see your good works, and glorify your Father who is in heaven."

—Matthew 5:16

Take a Tour of Cochise County

Cochise County Benson, Bisbee, Douglas, Sierra Vista, Tombstone, Willcox (and much more)	http://www.discoverseaz.com/ http://www.desertaura.com/
Douglas, Arizona	http://www.douglasaz.gov/ http://en.wikipedia.org/wiki/Douglas, Arizona
Douglas High School	http://www.hs.douglasschools.org/
Grand Theatre, Douglas	http://www.grandtheatredouglas.org/
Agua Prieta, Sonora, Mexico	http://www.justcoffee.org/index.shtml http://www.apsoncezar.com/
Slaughter's Ranch (San Bernardino Ranch)	http://www.vtc.net/~sranch/
Kartchner Caverns, Benson, Arizona	http://www.desertusa.com/azkartchner/index.html

Take good care of this book. It might come in handy someday.